Stewardship economy 7

economic terms explained
and
bibliography

Julian Pratt

Published by

Editorial note

This book brings together previously unpublished material which Julian worked on alongside the summary book, *Stewardship Economy 1: private property without private ownership*. With the other five books in the series, it provides the additional material that lies behind the proposals and assertions made in book 1. Sadly, Julian died before the work was finished and the editing complete. Some examples are now out of date, and some of the references are not available.

Rosemary Field

September 2021

ISBN 978-1-4717-0174-0

Contents

Books in the series

Introduction   **1**

Section 1   Economic Terms   **3**

Section 2 Some economics explained   **57**

    Supply and Demand   57

    The Deadweight loss: Effect of Taxation on Production   71

Section 3 Bibliography and links   **77**

Books in the series

Stewardship Economy 1: private property without private ownership is the first book and provides an overall summary of the main ideas.

Stewardship Economy 2: Valuing land and managing transition sets out in some detail how to establish the market rent of land and how to make the transition from an ownership to a stewardship economy. It also considers how the revenue from stewardship fees might be distributed.

Stewardship Economy 3: Land, environment and climate (this book) explores how a stewardship economy would transform the way we use land, provide housing and develop our cities. It goes on to consider how stewardship would help address pressing environmental and climate concerns.

Stewardship Economy 4: The economy, wealth and universal income focuses on the impact of stewardship on the national and global economy, how the distribution of wealth would be changed and the impact of a Universal Income.

Stewardship Economy 5: efficient, fair taxes and the role of the state describes the some of the adverse effects of our current system of taxation and considers the role of the state in a stewardship economy. It also explains some basic economic principles and terms.

Stewardship Economy 6: property rights describes the systems of property rights in our current economic system, their history and how property rights could be more fair and efficient in a stewardship economy.

Stewardship Economy 7: some economics explained, economic terms and bibliography. This book provides an introduction to some key economic concepts for the non-specialist and lists the references, as far as they are available.

Introduction

Section 1 of this book explains most of the terms used in this book and others in the Stewardship Economy series. Section 2 explores in more detail the concepts of supply and demand in the market economy and the deadweight loss of taxation.. Section 3 includes the bibliography for the whole series of Stewardship books.

Section 1 Economic Terms

Note: While most references are provided as footnotes to the text in this section, others are included in the bibliography in section 3.

Ad valorem

A tax or fee that varies with the value of property, products or services (such as a sales tax, VAT, inheritance tax, Land Value Tax) c.f. a 'unit tax' which is a fixed sum payable on each unit (for example, of sales).

Affordable housing

Housing that is affordable to people on low incomes. This includes housing that costs less than 3.5 - 4 times household earnings to purchase or 30% of earnings to rent.

The government uses a slightly different definition: 'housing provided to specified eligible households whose needs are not met by the market'. Affordability is determined with regard to local incomes and local house prices, and affordable housing should remain at an affordable price for future eligible households. By definition it does not include housing available on the open market, either for rent or purchase. It includes social renting, shared equity and can include both private sector and unsubsidised homes (Department for Communities and Local Government 2010:25)[1].

Aggregate demand

The total demand expressed in the economy.

Aid (international)

The gift of wealth from high-consumption economies to low-consumption economies.

---

[1]https://www.housinglin.org.uk/_assets/Resources/Housing/Policy_documents/PPS3.pdf accessed 19.10.2020 page 10

Allocative efficiency (also known as Pareto efficiency)

A situation in which no reorganisation or trade could raise the utility or satisfaction of one individual without lowering the utility or satisfaction of another individual (Paul Samuelson & William Nordhaus 1992:729). [2]

Under certain very specific circumstances, a free market is theoretically capable of guiding the production and distribution of wealth in a way that is efficient (in the sense of Pareto optimal) though not necessarily fair. This is summarised in the first theorem of welfare economics:

'A perfectly competitive, general-equilibrium market system will display allocative efficiency. In such a system, all goods' prices are equal to their marginal costs, all factor prices are equal to the value of their marginal products, and there are no externalities. Under these conditions, when each producer maximises profits and each consumer maximises utility, the economy as a whole is efficient; you cannot make anyone better off without making someone else worse off' (Paul Samuelson & William Nordhaus 1992:292)[3].

The rationale is discussed in detail in standard economic textbooks (e.g., Paul Samuelson & William Nordhaus 1992:293)[4]. The first theorem is based on a number of assumptions:

One assumption is that the economy is in a state of general equilibrium, in which supply and demand always come into equilibrium. This static model provides a very inadequate description of the dynamics of the economy, which behaves more like a complex adaptive system than a simple mechanical one (Paul Ormerod 1994)[5]. General equilibrium is a simplifying assumption, but it does make it possible to provide limited and short-term insights into isolated elements of the economy, and sometimes even into the workings of the system as a whole.

---

[2] Samuelson, Paul & Nordhaus, William (1992 (14th edition)) *Economics* New York McGraw-Hill

[3] Ibid

[4] Samuelson, Paul & Nordhaus, William (1992 (14th edition)) *Economics* New York McGraw-Hill

[5] Ormerod, Paul (1994) *The death of economics* London Faber & Faber

Another assumption is the separation of production (by firms) from consumption (by individuals and households). It assumes that firms will behave rationally and will choose to maximise profit, while individuals and households will behave rationally and maximise utility.

Maximisation of profit means that a firm will choose to produce the quantity of goods at which the difference between benefit and cost is maximal, which is when marginal net benefit equals marginal net cost.

Amenity

A site that that is consumed directly rather than being transformed through the process of production – for example, wilderness, recreation space and sites with views, natural beauty or spiritual significance. A site may serve as an amenity either if it can be accessed by the public or if it benefits neighbouring sites.

Amortise

To reduce a debt by paying small regular amounts (for example, for accounting purposes the value of a machine may be amortised over its estimated useful life).

Artefacts

Things that have been produced by people.

Asset

Some form of wealth – in particular, goods, stocks, shares (equities) and land.

Bads

In the parlance of tax shifting, things that we want to discourage like environmental damage c.f. goods.

Bank

A bank is an intermediary between depositors (savers) and borrowers (retail banking). Most banks take on additional functions, particularly creation of new money as debt (commercial banking), raising finance for clients and dealing in financial instruments (investment banking).

Benefit: cost ratio (BCR)

The ratio of the benefits of a project or investment to its costs.

Benefit trap

A financial incentive structure, created by the marginal rates of taxation and withdrawal of benefits, that would be expected to deter people who are receiving benefits from seeking work.

Betterment

Amount of increase in the value of land due to the development prospects (Owen Connellan 2004: p79).[6]

Brown

Political and economic approaches that are not green – in particular that accept high rates of discounting in benefit : cost calculations and ignore the perspective of other species and the ecosystem as a whole.

Brownfield

The term 'brownfield' is used in different ways:

1. Equivalent to previously developed land (PDL) - land on which there has, at some time, been buildings.

2. Land and buildings that are derelict, vacant or occupied and have been identified as having development potential. This potential may be limited by physical or regulatory constraints (English Partnerships 2006:9) [7].

3. In the USA the term is restricted to land that has been contaminated.

Bubble

Asset price increases that cannot be explained by changes in the fundamentals.

---

[6] Connellan, Owen (2004) *Land Value Taxation in Britain: Experience and opportunities* Cambridge, Massachusetts Lincoln Institute of Land Policy

[7] English Partnerships (2006) *The brownfield guide: a practitioner's guide to land re-use in England.*

www.englishpartnerships.co.uk/landsupplypublications.htm This link no longer operates because it was replaced by the Homes and Communities Agency in 2008.

Business

A person, or organised group of people, that transforms matter, energy and information from one state into another with the goal of making a profit (Eric Beinhocker 2005:280) [8].

Cadastral Survey

Strictly this refers to a survey of lands to serve as a basis of taxation (Shorter Oxford English Dictionary)[9]. More loosely, a survey on a scale showing the extent and measurement of every plot of land, providing a public register of the quantity, value and ownership of the real property of a country.

Capital

The term 'capital' can be used with qualification to describe stocks of assets or resources that contribute to production:

- 'produced capital' (also called 'physical capital') including machinery, equipment, infrastructure, buildings, improvements and other artefacts

- 'natural capital' including cropland, grazing land, forests, subsoil resources, fisheries

- 'human capital', which includes:

  o individual capital (also called 'human capital') such as knowledge and skills and the ability and willingness to make use of them

  o intellectual capital such as knowledge and ways of doing things

  o social capital such as relationships, trust and willingness to co-operate and work together for common purposes

  o institutional capital, the aspects of governance that contribute to production. Six dimensions have been identified – political stability and absence of violence; rule of law (including property rights

---

[8] Beinhocker, Eric (2005/2007) *The origin of wealth* London Random House

[9] Shorter Oxford English Dictionary (1975) London Oxford University Press

and an effective judicial system); government effectiveness; control of corruption; regulatory quality; voice and accountability (Kaufmann Kraay & Mastruzzi 2005)[10].

'Capital', as a factor of production, is also used to refer more narrowly just to 'produced capital' as defined above. When it takes this meaning, payments for the use of capital are called interest.

Capital goods

All that exists in the world as a result of past human activity. It includes capital goods that can be moved around (seeds, tools, machines, stores and supplies, computer programs, vehicles) and capital goods that are fixed to the land (buildings, crops, drainage systems). These fixed capital goods may also be described as improvements.

Capital value

The capital value of an asset (land, goods, stocks or shares) is the price at which it is bought and sold in an open market. Note that land can have a 'capital value' even though it is not 'capital' or 'capital goods'.

Capitalisation

Process whereby the value of an income stream (including any impact of taxation) is converted into the capital value of an asset.

Capitalise

To compute the present capital value of an asset based on the income that it is expected to give rise to.

Charge

A charge, such as a fee, is a payment for receiving some identifiable benefit.

---

[10] Kaufmann D, Kraay A & Mastruzzi M (2005) Governance matters IV: Governance indicators for 1994-2004 (Policy research working paper 3630) Washington DC World Bank

Citizen

The rank and status of citizen arose in the city states of ancient Greece. It signifies both the membership of a political community and the particular political form that is constitutional government. This is characterised by the sovereignty of the people by contrast with the sovereignty of a king or absolute government, whose people are referred to as subjects, not citizens.

The subgroup of the population admitted to citizenship has expanded over the course of time. Greek states excluded resident aliens, while the Roman republic allowed a selected group of aliens to become naturalised citizens. Slaves have always been excluded, and thus were excluded from the freedoms guaranteed by the US constitution. In certain times and places infants, women and people who fail to meet a criterion of property ownership have been excluded.

The term citizen thus comes to be used to describe people who possess political liberty and equality as the natural consequence of having been born human.

Civic bond

The ethic, voluntarily assumed but sustained by law, shared by citizens of a civic order (after Selbourne)[11].

Civic order (of a nation or city)

Communities of a given place ordered under a common rule as a polity, or a united body politic. The civic order embraces and is superior to all other associations within its bounds, and in the form of the nation is sovereign, a sovereignty which resides in the entire citizen-body (after Selbourne) [12].

Collateral

Property provided by a borrower to a lender that may be forfeited in case of default on a loan.

---

[11] Selbourne, David (2001) *Principle of duty*   Notre Dame Indiana Notre Dame press

[12] Selbourne, David (2001) *Principle of duty*   Notre Dame Indiana Notre Dame press

Common(s)

Property is said to be held in common when more than one person has rights to use it and exclude others from it.

(1) The word 'common' has been used since at least the 15th century to mean 'the undivided land held in joint occupation by a community'.

(2) It has acquired the additional meaning of 'unenclosed or waste land'.

Common land

Common land in the UK is generally held in private ownership, but subject to certain rights vested in others who are registered under the Common Registration Act of 1965 as 'commoners'.

Common property

Common property is held and managed by a defined community of commoners. They exclude others from using it; usage and extraction are regulated and allocated using often complex rules, norms and decision-making processes. Commons rely on the commoners' capacity to self-organise rather than on control exerted by a private property-owner or by the state.

Common-pool resource

A common-pool resource is a natural or man-made resource system from which it is costly to exclude users – for example a lake, pasture or irrigation system. It may be held as private property, collective property, common property or as an open access regime (after Elinor Ostrom 1990:30)[13].

Community

A voluntary association of people, commonly settled in a given place, held together by ties such as extended familial relationships, combined interest and purpose and shared memory, belief, values custom and knowledge (after Selbourne)[14].

---

[13] Ostrom, Elinor (1990) *Governing the commons: the evolution of institutions for collective action* Cambridge, UK, Cambridge University Press.

[14] Selbourne, David (2001) *Principle of duty* Notre Dame Indiana Notre Dame press

Complexity economics

An approach to economics that draws on the science of complex dynamic systems rather than equilibrium systems.

Computer assisted mass appraisal (CAMA)

The process of assessing, for purposes of taxation, the values of a large number of properties. Based on the principle of hedonic pricing, it enables the valuer to estimate the value of both buildings and land for all properties by comparing them with 'beacon' properties of known value (Tony Vickers 2009: 54) [15].

Concept / conception

A concept is an abstract idea. A conception of that concept is a concrete realisation of the idea in a particular society (Jeremy Waldron 1988:52)[16]

Conservatives

Conservatives seek to retain the best of what has gone before. They value the accepted social arrangements, which they see as necessary for an ordered society. They believe that change should be gradual not revolutionary.

Their preferred economic system may be libertarian with an emphasis on market mechanisms and resisting redistributive taxation; or they may prefer a more planned and directed economy.

Consumer Price Inflation

The rate of price inflation is the annual percentage increase in the price of a representative basket of goods and services purchased by consumers.

The best-known basket of goods and services is the Retail Price Index (RPI). After the ejection of the UK from the European Exchange Rate Mechanism in 1992, the Treasury adopted the policy of explicitly targeting the rate of inflation. Its chosen

---

[15] Vickers, Tony (2009) *Visualising the landvaluescape: developing the case for Britain* www.landvaluescape.org/archives/2009/12/visualising-landvaluescape-for-britian-thesis-published.html Kingston University (PhD thesis)

[16] Waldron, Jeremy (1988) *The right to private property* Oxford Clarendon press

measure was the RPIX – the RPI with mortgage interest payments stripped out.

In 2003 the targeted measure of inflation was changed from the RPIX to the Consumer Prices Index (CPI), which includes no measure directly related to house prices.

Corporation

A corporation is an entity that exists in law independently of its owners and employees, and has rights and responsibilities under the law. It is granted its incorporation by the state (for example, the BBC). The term is now generally used in its American sense to refer to an entity that conducts business, synonymous with the British term 'limited liability company'. The owners and employees are protected from the liabilities of the corporation.

Cost : Benefit ratio

see Benefit : Cost ratio.

Cost-effectiveness

The cost-effectiveness of an intervention is its cost divided by the objectives it achieves – $X for a man on the moon, £Y per job created.

Cultural commons

The cultural commons are those creations of the individual mind and the culture that are held as common property. The term is used in contrast to 'intellectual property rights'.

Cultural services

One of the sorts of benefits that we derive from the environment. They include peace, quiet, spirituality, wildlife, naturalness, space to walk, play, learn or just to be.

Deadweight loss (or excess burden) of taxes

The loss of economic activity caused by taxes. See section 2 for Effect of Taxation on Production and Rent.

Demand

The willingness and ability to pay a sum of money for some amount of a particular good or service (Penguin Dictionary of Economics).[17.]

Depression

A downturn in economic activity that is more severe and longer-lasting than a recession. It is usually recognised when the Gross Domestic Product falls by 10% or more.

Differential rent

Rent that arises because of the non-homogenous nature of land, with higher levels of differential rent arising on the most productive and desirable land (Brian Hodgkinson 2008:77) [18].

Discounting

Most people consider that the value of something at some time in the future (income, wealth, costs) is less than the same thing now. We discount this future by a discount factor. We can calculate from this an annual discount rate.

Distribution (of wealth)

The distribution of the produce of a society among its individual members (Shorter Oxford English Dictionary)[19] .

Easement

A right that somebody has to use or control land that is the property of another – for example a right of way or drainage rights.

Economic efficiency

see Efficiency, economic

---

[17] The Penguin Dictionary of Economics (1984) Harmondsworth Penguin

[18] Hodgkinson, Brian (2008) *A new model of the economy* London Shepheard-Walwyn

[19] Shorter Oxford English Dictionary (1975) London Oxford University Press

Economic good

Anything, whether a physical commodity or a service, which yields utility and which could command a price if bought or sold on a market (Penguin Dictionary of Economics)[20].

Economic rent

The amount paid to a factor of production over and above that which is necessary to keep it in production.

Economics

Science of the production and distribution of wealth (Shorter Oxford English Dictionary)[21].

Ecosystem

A system made up of organisms interacting in their physical environment.

Ecosystem services

Services that are provided by the natural environment that benefit people.

Eco-taxes

Taxes based on a physical unit (or proxy for it) of something that has a proven, specific negative impact on the environment (Owen Connellan 2004:178) [22].

Effectiveness

Something is said to be effective if it achieves what it intends to achieve (its objectives) – for example, to put a man on the moon or create jobs.

Technical effectiveness - an effective provider delivers the products they set out to deliver.

The effectiveness of a policy intervention or development project is the extent to which it achieves its objectives.

---

[20] The Penguin Dictionary of Economics (1984) Harmondsworth Penguin

[21] Shorter Oxford English Dictionary (1975) London Oxford University Press

[22] Connellan, Owen (2004) *Land Value Taxation in Britain: Experience and opportunities* Cambridge, Massachusetts Lincoln Institute of Land Policy

The effectiveness of a tax is the extent to which it raises revenue without imposing a deadweight burden on the economy.

The effectiveness of a benefit system is the extent to which it relieves poverty without discouraging people from playing an active part in the economy or discouraging people from taking appropriate responsibility for themselves.

The effectiveness of land use is the extent to which it is allocated to those who can make best use of it.

The effectiveness of a labour market is the extent to which it allocates work to those who want to work.

An effective financial market is one in which assets are traded at their market price and in which these prices reflect the underlying value of the assets.

Efficiency

'Efficient is a cheerful word put to many uses. A good pump is efficient; it moves the most water for the least energy. A portfolio is efficient if it produces the most profit at the least risk' (Mandlebrot & Hudson 2004 p.65)[23].

Efficiency is the ratio of useful outputs to inputs. For an engine the output is useful work and the input is the energy content of the fuel.

Technical efficiency is the ratio of outputs to inputs – energy efficiency is a measure of outputs to energy inputs, for example. A technically efficient provider can deliver the same products or services as a less efficient one at a lower cost, or better products or services for the same cost.

The efficiency of a policy intervention or development project is the ratio of its benefits to its costs – the benefit:cost ratio.

Efficiency of allocation. If allocating wealth, goods or production in a different way could improve one individual's position without harming anybody else – that is to say that the original allocation it is not Pareto optimal – the same inputs could result in a greater

---

[23] Mandelbrot, B. B. and Hudson, R. L. (2004) *The (Mis)Behavior of Markets: A Fractal View of Risk, Ruin and Reward.* New York: Basic Books

output of utility. For this reason, Pareto optimality is a measure of allocative efficiency.

Efficiency of tax collection is the ratio of the tax actually recovered to the tax that should be available for collection minus the costs of collection and the tax lost through avoidance and evasion. The costs of collection include the costs to government and to individuals and firms.

The efficiency of a tax is the amount of revenue it delivers for the government divided by the sum of this revenue and the deadweight loss.

The efficiency of benefit collection is the proportion of the resources which are available for distribution that reach the intended recipients.

The efficiency of land use is the extent to which land is used in a way that is judged to be productive. It is probably most helpful if this judgement about productivity takes any planning requirements as given – so a plot of land designated for use as a park is productive if it is in use as a park.

The efficiency of the land market is the extent to which this market allocates land efficiently.

The efficiency of a labour market is the proportion of people who look for employment who are able to find it.

Economic efficiency is used in this book in a rather all-encompassing way to refer to the maximisation of outputs for a given level of inputs.

For an economist, outputs (or ends) and inputs (or means) are measured using their monetary value. The valuations that count are the valuations of those who are willing and able to support their preferences by offering money – that is the nature of economics and the price mechanism (Paul Heyne [24]

Economic efficiency is subdivided into efficiency over different time-periods:

- Short-term efficiency: including allocative efficiency, efficient taxation, efficient land use and an efficient labour market

---

[24] Heyne, P. https://www.econlib.org/library/Enc/Efficiency.html

- Medium-term efficiency: the efficient use of land, labour and capital over an economic cycle of 15-20 years

- Long-term efficiency: the efficient unfolding of innovation, technology and economic growth over the long term.

Elastic

- see Elasticity

Elasticity

The percentage change in one variable divided by the percentage change in another variable. So the price elasticity of supply of land is the percentage by which the amount of land supplied changes when its price changes by 1%.

Emergent property

A property that is present at one level of organisation in a system that cannot be predicted at a lower level – for example, the behaviour of a family cannot be predicted from a knowledge of its individual members.

Eminent domain

The power of the state to take private property for public use.

Entail

Legally to limit inheritance of real property to a line or class of heirs.

Entrepreneur

An entrepreneur is a person who promotes innovation and change. The entrepreneur becomes aware of a possibility within the market such as goods or services that could be produced that are new or better or cheaper or more acceptable. They then bring together the other factors of production and wealth is created. Until other entrepreneurs catch up and begin to compete they are able to earn a higher level of profit than is absolutely required by the other factors of production and this excess profit is the reward of the entrepreneur.

Although it is at times useful to consider the entrepreneur as a separate factor of production, in this account the entrepreneur is considered to be a human factor of production and included within the heading of labour. Payments to the entrepreneur from excess profits is included within the term wages.

Environment

'Environment' is used to refer to all the natural world that is not 'land'. It may consist of amenities, resources and sinks. It covers all aspects of the natural world and includes

- bodies of water such as oceans, seas, lakes and rivers

- spaces below the surface such as the sea bed, aquifers, deposits of minerals and hydrocarbons and the spaces occupied by underground railways, cables, drains and so on

- spaces above the surface – the electromagnetic spectrum, the atmosphere, the ozone layer, airspace, satellite orbits and indeed the whole of the solar system – but not the space occupied by buildings or improvements attached to the land.

Environmental Dividend

The payment to each individual of equal shares of the revenue from the auction of the permits for the use of renewable resources.

Equities

Shares in a company that grant a claim on a proportion of the ownership of that company's profits and assets.

Equity

1. Equity is used to mean 'fairness'. It is about justice not sameness; it is healthy and inevitable that things are different, individual and personal. But equity does mean minimising unfair differences between individuals and communities – distributional fairness.

2. Equity is also used to refer to the value of an asset after all liabilities against it have been paid.

Even if the market is able to *allocate production and consumption efficiently*, this does not imply that it will *distribute production and consumption fairly*. There are many equilibrium positions that are Pareto optimal (on the 'production possibility frontier') and yet deeply unequal.

Equilibrium occurs at the intersection of the supply and demand curves; the demand curve is the aggregate demand curve for all households. Since demand is the willingness *and ability* to pay for a particular good or service, aggregate demand reflects disproportionately the interests of the wealthy.

If we want to achieve distributional fairness, and if this is to be achieved by market mechanisms, disposable income must first be distributed fairly (whatever that is taken to mean) amongst all individuals. If this can be achieved, the market may be expected to distribute fairly as well as allocate efficiently – or at least better than any central planner might manage.

Externalities

An economic transaction is usually based on a voluntary contract between two or more parties. 'Externalities' are any impacts (costs or benefits) that this activity has on people other than those making the contract. This it does not include impacts transmitted through the price mechanism.

Externalities can be thought of as activities that affect others for better (external economies) or worse (external diseconomies), without those others paying or being compensated for the activity (Paul Samuelson & William Nordhaus 1992)[25]

The term externality is used to describe activities that affect others for worse (negative externalities) or better (positive externalities), without those others being fully compensated. Where there are externalities, a person (or firm) makes decisions about how much to produce or consume without taking into account the effect of this on others. Where there are no externalities, a person (or firm) takes full account of the effect of their decisions on others.

A local shop may provide a social function as a meeting place; a theatre may bring in business for neighbouring restaurants; a park may increase the value of surrounding property. Any of these may fail because they are not able to capture for themselves the very real benefits (positive externalities) that they provide for others.

---

[25] Samuelson, Paul & Nordhaus, William (1992 (14th edition)) *Economics* New York McGraw-Hill

An important example is the provision of public transport, for example from commuter areas into the city centre. Because this enterprise cannot internalise the external benefits to homeowners, which are reflected in the increased market rents of the suburban houses, it may not be financially viable.

More important than external benefits (for environmental protection issues) are external costs - a factory that emits smoke and fumes that harm local property and public health, for example. The producer does not pay for these costs – they are borne by others (externalised).

Environmental economics relies on the price mechanism to tackle pollution by recognising costs of production that have been shifted (externalised) and requiring the producer to provide compensation (internalise them). In this way the firm's decisions come to be based on the true costs, including the costs to society not just the costs to the firm. For this to happen, those (who make up society) that bear the costs of the pollution must be recognised as having a claim against the polluter, and they must be able to collect a charge from the polluter that equals the shifted (externalised) cost.

Factors of production

Classical economics identifies the involvement of three factors in the process of production - land, labour and capital. Sometimes entrepreneurship is considered to be a separate factor of production. Production refers to the creation of goods or services for the purposes of sale or exchange.

When production occurs and wealth is created, each of the factors of production will have a claim on this wealth which will be shared amongst them. The share accorded to land is called rent; the share accorded to labour is called wages; and the share accorded to capital is called interest.

Fee

(a) A fee or charge is a payment to secure a particular benefit – by contrast with a tax, which is paid to raise revenue for the state.

'Stewardship fee' – see 'Stewardship fee'

(b) Fee (Feu, Fief, Feud). In feudal law, an estate in land held on condition of homage or service to a superior lord (later, this service was replaced by a return of grain or money) (Shorter Oxford English Dictionary)[26].

(c) In common law, an estate of inheritance of land (in English law understood to be feudally held of the crown; in the USA the holder of the fee is the absolute owner of the land) (Shorter Oxford English Dictionary)[27].

Fee simple

An estate in land held as an absolute and rightful possession, without any feudal obligations.

Firm

One or more businesses controlled in common by a person or group of people (Beinhocker 2005).

Fiscal policy

Government policy relating to taxation and spending.

Fixed asset

Produced assets that are themselves used repeatedly or continuously in the production process for more than one year. They comprise buildings and other structures, vehicles and other plant and machinery, also plants and livestock which are used repeatedly or continuously in production, for example, fruit trees or dairy cattle. They also include intangible assets such as computer software and artistic originals (Office for National Statistics 1998: p.628)[28].

Freedom

See Liberty

---

[26] Shorter Oxford English Dictionary (1975) London Oxford University Press

[27] Shorter Oxford English Dictionary (1975) London Oxford University Press

[28] ONS (Office for National Statistics) (1998) *National accounts: concepts, sources and methods* London

Free-rider

Somebody who gets some goods or services legally but without paying; somebody who consumes more than their fair share of a public good.

Fuel poverty

A household is said to be fuel poor if it needs to spend more than 10 per cent of its income on fuel to maintain an adequate level of warmth (Department of Energy and Climate Change) 29

Fundamental

The 'fundamental' value of an asset is the capitalisation of future expected income from that asset. It can be thought of as the sum of money you would have to invest today to provide you with an income stream equal to that expected income.

Gazetteer

The National Land and Property Gazetteer (NLPG) is a constantly updated address list that provides unique identification of properties in England and Wales. It is collated from Local Land and Property Gazetteers (LLPGs) that have been created by all councils with a statutory street naming and numbering function. Scotland has a National Gazetteer.

Gift economy

An economy in which people make gifts to each other of both goods and services. C.f. hidden economy

GINI coefficient

A measure of income inequality. A GINI coefficient of 0 indicates that a society has perfect equality – everybody receives the same income. A GINI coefficient of 1 indicates perfect inequality – one person receives all the income.

Goods

(a) 'Goods' are physical objects that are traded. *C.f.* 'services' which are also traded but where this does not involve the transfer of an object.

---

[29] Department of Energy and Climate Change (2011) Annual Report on Fuel Poverty London National Statistics Publication

(b) In the language of tax shifting, things that we want to encourage, such as earnings, profits and adding value, are called 'goods'. c.f.. 'bads'.

Grandfathering

Gifting environmental permits to firms that have been using that aspect of the environment in the past.

Greenfield

Land on which there has never been buildings.

Greens

The political and economic concerns of greens are as broad as those of other persuasions, but what characterises them is a particular concern for the environment, seeing the earth's ecosystem as a whole. They emphasise the importance of tackling threats to that ecosystem, particularly as a result of pollution and environmental destruction. They give considerable weight to the wellbeing of other species. The most significant characteristic is their refusal to accept the exponential discounting approaches of neoclassical economics.

Gross Domestic Product (GDP)

The total annual value of all goods and services produced in an economy.

Ground rent

An annual sum of money paid by a leaseholder to a freeholder for the use of the land on which the property stands.

Hectare

10,000 square metres, equivalent to 2.47 acres

Hedonic pricing

A way to reveal people's preferences for some attribute where there is no market for it. In principle, two properties are compared that are similar in all ways except for the presence or absence of that attribute – noise for example. The difference in land prices between the two properties is attributed to the preference for quiet. In practice a regression model is used to identify the average price of the attribute in a large set of properties with a range of attributes.

Hidden economy

Economic activity that is hidden from the authorities, for example to avoid regulation or taxation. (cf. informal economy).

High-consumption economy

In the stewardship economy books this term refers to the 65 countries that meet World Bank criteria for a 'high-income' economy – a per capita Gross National Income that was greater than $11,455 in 2007.

This term is used in preference to the term 'high-income' to stress the consumption implications of high per capita GNI, and in preference to 'developed country' with its implications that development is necessarily good.

c.f. Low-consumption economy and medium-consumption economy

Highest and best use (HABU)

A valuer assesses the value of a plot of land by comparing it with other similar plots of land, the value of which have been established in the market. These comparables are chosen to exemplify uses that generate the greatest net earnings that are physically possible, legally permissible and economically feasible – the highest and best use.

Homelessness

Legally, a person is homeless if they do not have a legal right to occupy accommodation, or if their accommodation is unsuitable to live in. This may include having no accommodation at all; having accommodation that is unsuitable, for example because of violence or for health reasons; living in a squat; and having been evicted.

Hypothecation

A tax or charge is said to be hypothecated when its revenue is earmarked, or pledged, for a particular use – the TV licence to fund public service broadcasting, a congestion charge to fund public transport.

Improvement

Changes to the land and environment that have been brought about by people – for example buildings, drainage, irrigation systems, roads, bridges.

Indigenous peoples

Ethnic groups who are native to a particular place on Earth and live or lived in an interconnected relationship with the natural environment there for many generations prior to the arrival of non-Indigenous peoples. (Wikipedia) [30].

Individual

One of several parts that make up a whole.

Inelastic

The supply (or demand) for something is said to be inelastic when the amount supplied (or demanded) does not depend on its price - see Elasticity

Inequality

There are a number of ways of measuring income inequalities in an economy, such as the ratio of the incomes of the top and bottom 10% of the population; or the GINI coefficient, which measures the degree of income inequality in the whole population.

Inflation

The inflation rate is the percentage annual increase in a price level. When the term is used without qualification it refers to consumer price inflation and the price level is that of a standard basket of consumer prices. Asset price inflation is the percentage annual increase in price level of land or shares.

Inflation is a feature of times when money supply has grown faster than the growth in production.

---

[30] https://en.wikipedia.org/wiki/Indigenous_peoples

Informal Economy

Economic activity undertaken by individuals or households with the primary objective of generating income and employment for those individuals.

C.f. hidden economy

Institution

'Institutions, within this framework [the economic analysis of institutions], are rules or procedures that prescribe, proscribe, or permit particular behaviour. Political institutions, as applied to economics, may define appropriate objects of exchange, the rules guiding the exchange process, and property rights with respect to both benefits and liabilities' (James Caporaso & David Levine 1992:149) [31].

Intellectual Property Rights

Intellectual property rights (IPR) are legally recognised exclusive rights to the use of creations of the mind – art, knowledge and ideas. These include patents for (novel, useful and non-obvious) inventions, copyright for artistic creations, trademarks and registered designs. Like other property rights, intellectual property rights confer rights of use and exclusion.

Defenders of the cultural commons contest this definition and would instead describe them as legally recognised monopoly privileges to the use of creations of the mind.

Interest

Interest is the payment for borrowing money.

Interest rate

The nominal interest rate is the percentage of a capital sum that a borrower pays a lender each year to borrow that sum.

The real interest rate is the nominal interest rate minus the inflation rate.

---

[31] Caporaso, James & Levine, David (1992) *Theories of political economy* Cambridge University Press

International stewardship

Arrangements whereby two or more countries pool the revenue from stewardship fees and/or environmental charges and distribute it between the two countries in proportion to their populations.

Investment

From the perspective of a household or firm, investment means the purchase of an asset with the intention that it will produce income or a capital gain.

From the perspective of the economy as a whole, each such purchase is counterbalanced by the sale of that asset. Investment, from this perspective, is used to refer to the creation of new capital goods such as plant and inventory – not to buying and selling existing capital goods or already existing land (see Paul Samuelson & William Nordhaus 1992:446)[32].

Keynesian

Relating to the theories of John Maynard Keynes, particularly his advocacy of monetary and fiscal policies to stimulate levels of demand in the economy.

Land

'Land' is used in these books to refer to the solid surface of the planet. It is characterised by its location. This differs from its usual meaning in economics and in law.

Stewardship Economy emphasises the fundamental distinction between three very different categories – people, artefacts (things made by people) and everything that occurs in nature without the intervention of people. The term 'natural world' is used to refer to this third category: all those sites, spaces, forces and opportunities that occur in nature without the intervention of people. The 'natural world' is divided into 'land' and 'the environment'. 'Land' is the solid surface of the planet. It includes agricultural, urban, residential, industrial, and commercial land, public spaces, highways, derelict sites, moorland and wilderness. Land comprises the location, described by its co-ordinates, and the topsoil.

---

[32] Samuelson, Paul & Nordhaus, William (1992 (14th edition)) *Economics* New York McGraw-Hill

This use of the term 'land' is close to the everyday common-sense use of the word, but different from its meanings in both law and economics. It is close to the way that it is used in writings on surveying and valuing and is probably what is meant by 'land' in the International Accounting Standard on Leases (IAS 7) although the term is not explicitly defined there. The Royal Institute of Chartered Surveyors[RICS 2006:7] defines land as location combined with the physical ability and legal right to use and construct improvements on the site. This differs from its use in economics, including writings on Land Value Taxation, where 'land' is used to mean what is referred to in a stewardship economy as the 'natural world' and includes the oceans, atmosphere, mineral reserves and so on.

It also differs from the legal meaning of 'land', which includes any changes ('improvements') brought about by people such as buildings, drainage, irrigation systems, roads and bridges. By contrast, a stewardship economy distinguishes improvements from 'land'. Most places are, in this terminology, a combination of 'land' and 'improvements'.

'Land' and 'the environment' refer to a space, to its potential use and to its naturally occurring contents. These may include natural resources (such as topsoil, water, minerals, fossil fuels, wild animals, naturally occurring plants and trees and biodiversity); sinks (space to dump household waste, sewage, industrial and agricultural pollutants, carbon dioxide, radioactive isotopes etc.); and amenities (aspects of the natural world that are consumed directly rather than being transformed through the process of production – things like natural beauty, views, sites of spiritual and cultural significance, wilderness, recreation space and so on.

There are several ways in which the stewardship economy books have assigned something to the category of 'artefact' (made by people) rather than 'the natural world' – or to 'land' rather than 'environment'. This borders on the arbitrary and is made for instrumental rather than principled reasons:

- ❑ The 'natural world' is nothing like a state of nature but has been shaped by people over the millennia. Improvements, such as drainage or land reclamation, are treated in a stewardship economy as gradually decaying in value until they can be considered to have become part of the natural world. This does not have to do with 'naturalness' but with the ownership claims that people can reasonably have

❑ This does not include cultivated plants, trees and farm animals as part of the 'natural world' or 'the environment' but as 'artefacts'. This is not intended to diminish their status as living beings but because it is appropriate for farmers to own these beings in a stewardship economy.

❑ The distinction between 'people' and 'the natural world' may also seem false. We are all part of nature. Why distinguish between, say, a dam made by a beaver and a dam made by humans? The reason that these books do so is to make it easier for us humans to sort out our thinking about our property claims to the natural world. Beavers have other ways of dealing with property.

❑ A small stream flowing through a plot of land, used only by the steward of that land, is considered to be part of that land. A river flowing through a plot of land, to which others have rights to abstract water, to travel, to fish and so on, is considered to be part of a network of water resources and so to be part of the environment. The classification of a larger stream is made by a regulatory body according to agreed criteria.

Land reform

A programme of redistributing the ownership of plots of land from large landowners to those who work and live on the land.

Land tax

This term is applied to any tax levied on land (c.f. Land Value Taxation).

Land tenure

Refers to the laws, customs and practices governing the rights, duties and relationships of people to the land. At the core of any system of land tenure is a property system.

Land Value Taxation

A method of raising public revenue by means of a tax or charge on some proportion of the market rent of land.

Land Value Taxation has this specific meaning and does NOT refer to any tax that falls on land – c.f.Land Tax.

Landlord

In an ownership economy a landlord is the owner of a property who leases it to a tenant.In a stewardship economy a landlord is the steward of a property who leases it to a tenant.

In both sorts of economy the tenant pays to the landlord a regular sum that is made up of two parts – the rent for the land (which a steward passes on by paying the stewardship fee) and a payment to lease the buildings and other improvements.

Landvaluescape

This term has been introduced by Tony Vickers to refer to a conceptual model of economic reality as it unfolds across space and time. It is often revealed in a computer visualisation but an expert can form a mental picture of the shapes and 'features' in landvaluescape without resort to computer models of valuation data (2009:13)[33].

Legal Positivism

A positivist approach holds that the truth of legal propositions consists of facts about the rules that have been adopted by specific social institutions, and in nothing else.

Legal title

The complex bundle of rights and responsibilities that describe the relationship between the possessor of property and others.

Liberal (classical)

Those who emphasise individual rights, personal freedoms and responsibilities, and representation rather than participation.

---

[33] Vickers, Tony (2009) *Visualising the landvaluescape: developing the case for Britain* www.landvaluescape.org/archives/2009/12/visualising-landvaluescape-for-britian-thesis-published.html Kingston University (PhD thesis)

Liberal democracy

Democracy that places the freedom of the individual at the centre of its concerns (David Selbourne) [34].

Liberal party

Political party, given its name by Lord John Russell, that grew out of the Whig Party. Its founding principles were religious liberty, the abolition of slavery, universal suffrage and free trade.

Liberals

The term 'liberal' is used with a confusing variety of meanings. In these books 'liberal' is used to refer to the 'new liberals', such as Thomas Hill Green, who emerged at the end of the 19th century. These thinkers developed a more expansive view of 'positive' liberty (*see* liberty) than the 'negative' freedom from interference by others (especially government) advocated by the classical or 19th century liberals like John Stuart Mill (*see* libertarians).

Liberals emphasise the importance of 'positive' liberty (the freedom of self-realisation), human rights and responsibilities and equality of opportunity. They give attention to the nature of relationships between people and between people and the state.

Their platform brought together market mechanisms, free trade and anti-trust laws with state funding for education and health care and a system of benefits for those in need.

Libertarians

In these stewardship economy books, 'libertarian' refers to those people who focus on the (negative) liberty of the individual from interference by others, particularly the state, and who are often referred to as classical liberals or 19th century liberals (*see* liberty).

Right-libertarians include John Locke and John Stuart Mill as well as Friedrich Hayek and Murray Rothbart. Left-libertarians, who advocate equal access to land and the environment, include Hillel Steiner.

---

[34] Selbourne, David (2001) *Principle of duty* Notre Dame Indiana Notre Dame press

The favoured economic system of the libertarian is the free market, where each person is responsible solely for his own choices. The individual is asked to act in their own self-interest, and it is assured that this will result in the maximum efficiency in the workings of the economy (or at least better than any planner could manage). It is based on the 17th century French doctrine of "Laissez-Faire", but its best-known formulation is to be found in the 'Wealth of Nations':

"Every individual endeavours to use his capital so that it may be of the greatest value. He neither knows nor intends to promote the public interest, nor knows how much he is promoting it. He intends only his own security, his own gain. And he is in this led by an invisible hand to promote an end which was no part of his intention. By pursuing his own interest he frequently promotes that of society more effectually than when he really intends to promote it" (Adam Smith, 1776)[35].

Libertarian supporters of the free market now contend that, beyond the fair operation of the market, responsibility to others is a matter of individual choice, not obligation. People with the means may or may not choose to help others in the spirit of charity.

Liberty

Liberty is not the unfettered licence to act without consideration of the effects on others **(John Stuart Mill 1859).** It is the sum of free choices open to an individual, provided they do not restrict the free choices of other individuals.

Liberty in this sense is 'freedom from', or negative liberty – freedom from arbitrary imprisonment, from expropriation of property and from violent attack. Positive liberty, 'freedom to', is a different matter. Democratic freedom is the right of people to participate in the process by which they are governed. Isaiah Berlin (1958) [36] makes clear that this positive liberty may not be reconcilable with 'negative liberty'. Supporters of negative liberty generally want to curb the state's authority while supporters of positive liberty want access to its exercise.

Liberty is not the same as fairness, or justice or equality. There are

---

[35] Smith, Adam (1776) *An inquiry into the nature and causes of the wealth of nations* Dublin Whitestone et al

[36] Berlin, Isaiah (1958) *Two concepts of liberty* Oxford Clarendon

trade-offs between each of these as well as the delicate balance between the liberties of different individuals.

Listed building

Building protected from any development that alters its historic features, as defined in detailed official lists (Owen Connellan 2004)[37].

Lost surplus

see Deadweight loss of taxes

Low-consumption economy

These books use this term to refer to the 49 countries that meet World Bank criteria for a 'low-income' economy – a per capita Gross National Income that was less than \$935 in 2007.

This term is used in preference to the term 'low-income' to stress the consumption implications of low per capita Gross National Income, and in preference to 'less-developed country' with its implications that development is good.

c.f. High-consumption economy and medium-consumption economy

Macroeconomics

The study of the economy of a country at an aggregate level.

Margin of production

The (extensive) margin of production is the least productive site on which anybody would choose to engage in production.

Marginal net benefit

The marginal net benefit is the benefit received by a firm when it increases output by one unit.

Marginal net cost

The marginal net cost is the cost to a firm of increasing output by one unit.

---

[37] Connellan, Owen (2004) *Land Value Taxation in Britain: Experience and opportunities* Cambridge, Massachusetts Lincoln Institute of Land Policy

Market

A market is a mechanism by which buyers and sellers of a commodity interact to determine its price and the quantity that is made available.

Market failure

Market failure describes inefficiencies that arise in markets from a variety of causes including externalities, under-provision of public goods and monopolies.

Market rent

The market rent of a plot of land, of a property comprising land and improvements such as buildings or of an aspect of the environment is the 'estimated amount for which a property should lease (let) on the date of valuation between a willing lessor and a willing lessee on appropriate lease terms in an arms-length transaction after proper marketing wherein the parties had each acted knowledgeably, prudently and without compulsion' (RICS 2009:42).[38]. It is equal to the opportunity cost of leaving vacant land (or unused natural resources) unused.

The market rent reflects the potential revenue from land when it is put to its highest and best permissible use and is not necessarily related to the rent that is being paid for its current use.

In the context of stewardship, the 'appropriate lease terms' refer to land or the environment but not to buildings and improvements; and include an indefinite duration, annual reviews, annual payments (as monthly instalments) and liability for any damage, pollution or other disimprovement to the land or environment.

It is easiest to determine the market rent of a plot of land when it has no buildings or other improvements on it. When the rent of unimproved land is established by offering it to the highest bidder in the open market, this sale determines the market rent of the land.

Market rent is also used to apply to a resource rent of some aspect of the environment. For example, the spectrum auctions revealed

---

[38] RICS (2009) *RICS Valuation standards (Red book)* London Royal Institute of Chartered Surveyors

the market rent, or resource rent, of those parts of the electromagnetic spectrum.

Market value

The market value – of a plot of land, of a property comprising land and improvements such as buildings or of an aspect of the environment – is the 'estimated amount for which a property should *exchange* on the date of valuation between a willing seller and a willing buyer in an arms-length transaction after proper marketing wherein the parties had each acted knowledgeably, prudently and without compulsion'.

Marriage value

The additional value that sometimes emerges when two interests in a property are combined. These may be the interests in two adjacent properties but are more usually a leasehold and freehold interest in the same property.

Medium-consumption economy

This term refers to the 95 countries that meet World Bank criteria for 'upper-middle-income' or 'lower-middle-income' economies – a per capita Gross National Income that was between $936 and $11,455 in 2007.

This term is used in preference to the term 'medium-income' to stress the consumption implications of high per capita Gross National Income, and in preference to 'emerging economy'.

c.f. High-consumption economy and low-consumption economy.

Microeconomics

The study of the economic behaviour of individuals and firms.

Monetary policy

The policy of a government or a central bank on the money supply and interest rates.

Money

Money is the medium of exchange employed when goods and services are bought and sold.

Monopoly

1. In economics a monopoly (literally a single seller) exists where an enterprise can control the supply of a particular product or service and so can determine its price.

A natural monopoly occurs in an industry when one firm can supply the whole market more cheaply than two or more firms; examples are distribution networks such as electricity, water and sewage.

2. In general speech monopoly refers to 'exclusive possession or control', 'exclusive ownership through legal privilege, command of supply or concerted action'. This is the sense in which the term is generally used in these books.

3. Monopoly ® is a board game in which properties are traded.

Moral hazard

The risk that a body will alter its behaviour because it is not fully exposed to the consequences of its actions.

Natural resources

The contents of the natural world that may be used in situ or, more usually, extracted – such as topsoil, water, minerals, fossil fuels, wild animals, naturally occurring plants and trees, and biodiversity.

Natural world

All the sites, spaces, forces and opportunities that occur in nature without the intervention of people. It is made up of land and the environment.

Nature

'The material world, or its collective objects or phenomena, the features and products of the earth itself, as contrasted with those of human civilisation' (Shorter Oxford English Dictionary)[39]

Negative liberty

See liberty

---

[39] Shorter Oxford English Dictionary (1975) London Oxford University Press

Net Domestic Product (NDP)

Gross Domestic Product minus the consumption of fixed capital.

Net energy ratio

The ratio of the energy that is productively released from an energy source to the energy consumed in its production.

Net present value

(NPV)

(a)The net present value of a resource is the total resource rent per unit of resource. It requires assumptions about future prices and costs of extraction, the rate of extraction and the discount rate [Kirk Hamilton 2007 p. 124]40.

(b) A measure of the overall value today of a stream of payments over time. The NPV is the amount that would need to be invested at a (nominal) commercial interest rate at the beginning of the period of payments such that, with accumulated interest, it would be just adequate to meet all the payments as they fall due.

See also Present Value and Years Purchase.

New land market

A proposed market in which all transfers are made through auctions conducted by the Land Stewardship Trust and all bids are for annual payments of rent.

Normative economics

(also known as welfare economics)

The study of what is right and wrong, what is desirable and what is undesirable, about the economy's functioning - the study of the best way to organise economic activity, the best distribution of income, and the best tax system. [Samuelson]41

---

[40] Hamilton, Kirk (2006) *Where is the wealth of nations? Measuring capital in the 21st century* Washington DC World

[41] Samuelson, Paul & Nordhaus, William (1992 (14th edition)) *Economics* New York McGraw-Hill

Owner-occupier

A person (or business) that owns its own home (or business premises).

Ownership

Ownership is widely used to describe the possessive relationship that is property. In these books, however, the use of the term is restricted to the particular form of private property relationship that is known as the liberal conception of ownership and is what we currently mean when we talk about owning a book or a house.

Ownership economy

An economy grounded in ownership of the natural world (c.f. stewardship economy).

Pareto optimality

An allocation of goods or wealth or income is described as efficient or Pareto optimal if 'no reorganisation could raise the utility or satisfaction of one individual without lowering the satisfaction of another individual' (Paul Samuelson & William Nordhaus). It is therefore an allocation in which no self-interested individual would veto a change from the status quo if they had the opportunity to do so. Pareto optimality is equivalent to a requirement for perfect consensus for change.

This may be a useful criterion because if a situation is *not* Pareto optimal, it can be altered so that at least one person improves their position without harming anyone else. Pareto optimality should be seen as necessary but not sufficient. Its disadvantages as a criterion are that:

o it is a measure of allocative efficiency but not of other sorts of efficiency

o it does not meet any particular criterion of fairness

o it tends to legitimise the status quo – for example in a two-person society in which A has all the wealth and B has none, any net transfer of wealth (i.e., without a balancing transfer of labour) from A to B, for example by taxation, is Pareto inefficient.

Peak Oil

Peak Oil is the time when the rate of extraction of oil reaches a peak.

Perfect competition

Perfect competition occurs when the following conditions are met:

- **Transferable property rights** – a set of transferable property rights must exist for all goods and bads, with the costs and benefits accruing to the owner.

- **Many buyers and sellers** - when a monopoly is present, a firm is able to set or manipulate the prices and quantities of goods and services in the market as a whole. Monopolies are absent when all households and firms act as price takers (prices reflect marginal costs). A monopolist can drive up prices, reducing the amount produced compared with a competitive market, and thereby increase profits.

- **Complete information** - all households and firms have complete information about goods and services offered in the market and their prices.

- **Markets are complete** – there are markets not just for bread (for example) here and now, but futures markets for bread at every place and time.

- **No distortion of prices by taxation** - the theorem assumes that prices reflect marginal costs. Any tax that alters prices (and this includes Income Tax, National Insurance Contributions and Corporation Tax as well as the more obvious VAT – indeed anything other than a Ramsay tax) distorts allocative efficiency and invalidates the first theorem.

- **No externalities** - the market mechanism will only produce allocative efficiency if all costs and benefits are included in the economic judgements. This is not possible where there are externalities.

- **No public goods** – it is assumed that society is no more than an aggregation of individuals and individual households – that is, that goods and services provided to society as a whole are not considered.

Although economics for a long time operated within the confines of these assumptions, there has been increasing interest in exploring the economics of situations in which one of them is relaxed. Many of the Nobel Prizes for economics since 2000 have been awarded for work in the areas that assume incomplete information, or human behaviours that are closer to those that people might actually use.

Plot

An area of the surface of the Earth with defined boundaries and co-ordinates (see also 'site).

Political perspectives

One way of making sense of the range of political perspectives that people adopt is by considering what they choose to give attention to.

A system, such as a society, is a whole that can be thought of as interconnected parts; these books suggest that libertarians tend to give attention to the parts (individuals), liberals to the connections (rights and duties) and socialists to the whole. Perhaps it is fanciful to think that libertarians focus particularly on liberté, liberals on egalité and socialists on fraternité.

A different lens is that of time. These books suggest that conservatives tend to give attention to the past (learning from the past, retaining the best bits and avoiding revolutionary change); greens tend to give attention to the future; and pragmatists to give attention to the present.

Positive law

The law that is formally adopted by the state.

Positive Liberty

See liberty

Poverty

Poverty is a state in which an individual or family receives a low income. 'Low' can be assessed either in absolute terms, below a certain threshold deemed to be adequate, or in relative terms, less than 60% of the median household income. The UK government uses both these measures in tracking child poverty, along with a measure that combines material deprivation with relative poverty.

Poverty trap

This may be used to refer to either the benefits trap or the unemployment trap.

Present value

(a) the price at which an asset is currently being bought and sold in the open market

(b) the discounted value of future net cash flows from an asset. The discount factor should reflect the cost of waiting (the pure time value of money), the risk of the asset and expected future inflation.

See also Net Present Value

Primary Goods

- see Goods

Primary health care

First point of access to health care.

Production

The creation of goods or services for the purposes of sale or exchange.

Products

Goods and services

Profits

Profit refers to the return to the entrepreneur or business for innovating, responding to market changes and taking risks. This is equal to the total revenue minus the operating expenses, wages, interest / dividends and rent.

In accounting terms a sole trader may not pay himself or herself a wage, and a landowner may not pay rent and both these notional amounts may appear in the accounts as profit . In economic terms, profit is the difference between total revenue and the total opportunity costs of all the resources used.

Progressive tax

The tax rate is lower on those with low income than on those with a higher income. C.f. regressive tax.

Property

(a) Something that is possessed. Anything with which people (and other legal entities) can have a possessive relationship can be described as property. So, for example:

Natural property is the world that is naturally present without the intervention of people.

Artefacts are things that have been produced by people.

(b) The concept of property. Property is also used to refer to the nature of this possessive relationship. So, for example:

Private property (*res privitae)* is property whose use and disposition is determined in relation to the wishes of an individual (or other legal entity).

Common property (*res communes*) is property whose use and disposition is determined in relation to the wishes of a defined group of people.

Collective property (*res publicae*) is property whose use and disposition is determined in relation to the wishes of the whole of society.

(c) 'A property'. This term is used to refer to something like a house or a farm made up of both land and improvements on that land.

Property system

A property system consists of a set of rules governing access to, and control of, artificial and natural property. Its purpose is to resolve problems of the allocation of property.

Public Goods

Goods that must be supplied communally because they cannot be withheld from one individual without withholding them from all.

A public good is a good that is consumed by society as a whole rather than by individuals. Its benefits are indivisibly spread amongst the entire community, whether or not individuals want to purchase it (Paul Samuelson & William Nordhaus 1992:311). Its key attribute is that it is non-rival in consumption – if one person consumes some of the good there is still plenty left for others. It can therefore be provided as cheaply to everyone as to one person.

Public goods have a second attribute – that they are non-excludable. This means that it is impossible, or prohibitively expensive, to exclude people from using the good. This means that it is not practically possible to charge for its use, so a price cannot be established. The usual examples that are given are street lighting and lighthouses – even though lighthouses in the UK are funded by a levy on ships using nearby harbours. Public goods are a challenge for markets because, to achieve allocative efficiency, the market mechanism has to aggregate individual demand to arrive at an aggregate demand curve and so at a price.

For rival consumption, once a price has been established each individual will choose how much, if any, of the good they will purchase (Michael Common 1978:102). For non-rival consumption, even if a price could be established, the idea of each individual choosing how much to pay is deeply problematic, and the government has to do the aggregation.

Economic theory suggests that we should ask each person what they would be willing to pay, and then actually charge them that amount (the Lindall price). One difficulty is that people who understand this approach would understate their willingness to pay and free-ride on others. Another is that it feels unfair and arbitrary to most people.

In practical terms the way to decide how much of a public good to provide is through political processes, not through economic reason.

Most externalities can be thought of in terms of public goods – pollution is a negative public good, or a public bad. The consumer cannot be excluded and so receives the good (or bad) without compensation. Its benefits are indivisibly spread amongst the entire community, whether or not individuals desire to purchase it. (Paul Samuelson & William Nordhaus 1992 p311)[42]

---

[42] Samuelson, Paul & Nordhaus, William (1992 (14th edition)) *Economics* New York McGraw-Hill

Quantitative easing

From 2009 the Bank of England carried out a programme called quantitative easing (QE) in which it issued new money electronically. This bypassed the fractional reserve banking system. The new money was used to purchase government debt (gilts) for money to be provided to the banks or to the government, and this was intended to lower long-term borrowing costs.

Radiative forcing

Radiative forcing is a measure of the influence that a climatic factor has in altering the balance of incoming and outgoing energy in the Earth's atmosphere system.

Rates

Local authority rates are a form of British property tax, formerly levied on homes but still levied on annual values on non-domestic properties (Connellan 2004)[43]

Real Estate

This term has been used to mean immovable property, such as lands and houses, since the mid-17th century.

There is disagreement about the meaning of 'real' in this context, as it was used in two different senses in the 16th century.

Derived from the Old French 'réel' and ultimately from the Latin 'res', a thing, 'real' was used in a legal sense. Real property, which passed on the owner's death to their heir, was distinguished from personal property that was recoverable by a personal action.

When derived from the Old French 'real', 'royal' also meant royal, regal, kingly – a usage we retain in terms like 'real tennis'.

The significance of this disagreement is how we think about the ownership of real estate. Under the feudal system land was royal domain and all land was held from the king. 'Title' was granted by the king and this conferred both nobility and property rights.

---

[43] Connellan, Owen (2004) *Land Value Taxation in Britain: Experience and opportunities* Cambridge, Massachusetts Lincoln Institute of Land Policy

Recession

A recession is a time when business activity is falling. It is usually recognised when there are two successive quarters in which growth in Gross Domestic Product is negative.

Regressive tax

The tax rate is applied uniformly, taking a larger percentage of income from those on low income than from those with a higher income. c.f. progressive tax.

Rent

Regular payments made for the use of any part of the natural world, particularly for the use of land. This differs from the way the term is used in an everyday and commercial sense, where the 'rent' of a property includes both *rent* for the use of land (the plot of ground, or site) and *rental* for the improvements (the bricks and mortar).

It also differs from the way that the term is used by economists. They apply the term 'economic rent', or just plain 'rent', not just to payments made for the use of land and the natural world but for anything that is scarce and cannot be produced in larger quantities at will (that is fixed in supply). Economists use the term 'rent' to refer to payments for a rare painting, the use of a patent or intellectual property, or a unique opera singer. They also refer to the super-normal profits that occur where there is imperfect competition as 'rent' [Robert Kuttner 1999:27]. The use of the term rent is restricted in these books to payments for the use of land and the environment, not to people (even when their contribution is unique) or artefacts (even where these are fixed in supply). So, rent refers to payments for the use of the natural world or, as Fred Harrison and James Robertson say, 'payments that people make for what they take from the value of common resources'.

See also economic rent, market rent, differential rent, scarcity rent and rental.

Rental

(1) Leasing

(2) The amount payable by the user of a *fixed asset* to its owner for the right to use that asset for a specified length of time (Office for National Statistics 1998: p 628) [44] .

Reserves (of minerals)

Mineral resources that are available at current market prices and with current technology.

Resources (of minerals)

The total amount of a mineral present in the earth's crust.

Resource rent

The revenue that can be generated from the extraction of a natural resource, less the cost of extracting the resource.

Scarcity rent

Rent that arises from the limited availability of even low quality land. This sort of rent would arise even where land is homogenous in quality, and so does not contribute to economic rent (Brian Hodgkinson 2008 p.77)[45].

Secondary goods

See Goods

Seigniorage

The revenue derived from putting legal tender into circulation. It is equal to the difference between the face value of the currency and its cost of production. For bank loans it is the interest paid on the loan that creates the credit.

Shadow economy

Hidden Economy

---

[44] ONS (Office for National Statistics) (1998) *National accounts: concepts, sources and methods* London

[45] Hodgkinson, Brian (2008) *A new model of the economy* London Shepheard-Walwyn

46

Site

For the purpose of stewardship the natural world is divided into 'sites' that each have a steward. The surface of the land mass of the earth is divided into plots of land, each of which is a 'site'. The term also includes other aspects of the natural world (for example, oceans, air, electromagnetic spectrum, satellite orbits) divided into parts that can have a relationship with a single steward.

SOCEF

Social Opportunity Cost of Exchequer Funds.

Social capital

Connections amongst individuals; social networks and the norms of reciprocity and trustworthiness that arise from.

Socialist

This title was first applied 1827 to followers of Robert Owen.

Socialists recognise a fundamental and explicit commitment by the state to take responsibility for all its members, in the same way that a family operates. This view was summarised by the early French socialist Louis Blanc:"Produire selon ses facultés et consmmer selon ses besions (From each according to his ability, to each according to his needs)" (1850:75)[46]

While recognising the importance of liberté and egalité it gives most attention to fraternité – or perhaps to sororité. Such a society attempts to guarantee that the necessities of life are provided for all people, and that society works in a way that is beneficial to all.

Traditionally, the only recognised way to intervene in complex systems was to re-design and re-engineer them. This often led socialists to advocate a command economy in which production and demand are shaped by planners not by the market, and in which social relationships are engineered.

Increased understanding of complex self-organising systems has resulted in some socialists taking a different approach. Interventions to improve society for all may instead involve altering individual and

---

[46] Blanc, Louis (1850 (9th edn)) *Organisation du travail* Paris Nouveau Monde LG Archive special Hutchinson 159

organisational 'rules of thumb' and, most fundamentally, the 'rules of the game' – like the property system.

Speculation

The purchase (or sale) of an asset in the hope that its price will rise (or fall).

State

The public arm and instrument of the civic order, acting on behalf, and in the interests of, the civic order. (after Selbourne [47])

Steward-occupier

A steward who occupies the land of which they are a steward – the equivalent of an owner-occupier in an ownership economy.

Stewardship

The term 'stewardship' describes a new relationship (in place of 'ownership') between a person (or group of people or an organisation) and a 'site'. A steward has the right to use the land, or site. They own (in the conventional sense) any improvements they make to the site and are responsible for any harm done to it. A steward is responsible for paying the annual market rent of the site as a stewardship fee.

The term steward is thought to be derived from 'sty-ward', a person who looks after farm animals. It has been consistently used to mean 'one who manages the affairs of an estate on behalf of his employer'. 'Stewardship' has been used more generally to describe a responsible approach to managing something on behalf of others – for example, a conservationist approach to the natural world, a sense of responsibility to other people, other species, future generations, God.

Many people would think of stewardship as managing the natural world on behalf of something greater than just humankind. 'Dark Greens' recognise our responsibility not just to humankind but to all living things and to Gaia herself – because they recognise that we are not separate from nature, but part of it [Ralph Metzner 1995:66]. People of

---

[47] Selbourne, David (2001) *Principle of duty*   Notre Dame Indiana Notre Dame press

faith may understand this responsibility in recognition of God's dominion over the world and the universe.

Each of these groups come to the word 'stewardship' with rather different assumptions. And the term is used with other meanings in other contexts. For example, Christians also use it to describe something quite different – the practice of tithing a proportion of income to the church. And the UK Department for Environment, Food and Rural Affairs (Defra) and Natural England administer an Environmental Stewardship Scheme that makes payments to farmers who protect and enhance the natural environment.

Nick Dennys[2002: 14] points out that if we are to bring about stewardship we need to celebrate, value and protect the environment and he suggests that democracy in valuation requires the use of market valuations.

> The steward of a part of the natural world has:

- o *the right of access* – to use it in the way that they choose, within the constraints of any relevant regulations

- o *the responsibility of care* – to manage it responsibly and husband it for future generations, accepting liability for any damage done to it

- o *the duty of compensation* – to pay an annual fee, equal to its market rent, into a fund that is used to benefit everyone.

- o *ownership*, in the conventional sense, of any buildings or other improvements.

We do not and cannot own the Earth but can, and must, act as its steward.

Stewardship economy

A stewardship economy is one in which the natural world is held in stewardship, and things made by people are held in ownership.

In a stewardship economy the income from stewardship fees may be used instead of conventional taxes as a source of revenue for the state or distributed to the whole population as a Universal Income. The income from environmental charges is distributed on an equal per capita basis as Environmental Dividend or invested for the benefit of future generations.

Stewardship fee

A stewardship fee is an annual fee that is paid to secure the stewardship of a plot of land, equal to its market rent.

A stewardship fee is a charge on the market rent of land. If the revenue were to be used as revenue for the state, it would be not a fee or charge but a Land Value Tax. Supporters of Land Value Taxation from time to time question whether the term conveys its intended meaning in the 21st century (Robert Andelson: 2000:xxiii). The term 'stewardship' is preferable for several reasons.

'Land Value Taxation' is used to refer to the collection of *any* proportion of the market rent of land – and people are usually talking about less than 25 per cent. 'Stewardship', on the other hand, points to the collection of 100 per cent of the market rent. It is helpful to have a term that always refers to this most radical end of the Land Value Tax spectrum – both because some supporters of Land Value Taxation would distance themselves from stewardship, which they think is too extreme to be of practical interest, and because methods of valuation that work well when less than 50 per cent of the market rent is collected cannot be used in a stewardship economy.

'Stewardship fee' avoids several other possible confusions that accompany the term Land Value Taxation. It avoids any confusion about the meaning of the term 'land'. Another is that the word 'value' seems to suggest to many people that the land itself has an intrinsic value, probably because the term 'Land Value Taxation' was introduced at a time when the agricultural sector was of much greater economic importance, markets for produce were more local and the 'original and indestructible powers of the soil' were as important as its location.

The term 'Stewardship fee' also has the advantage of avoiding the word 'tax', which should be reserved to mean 'income derived by the sovereign or state from its subjects or citizens'. The precise demarcation between a tax and a charge (or fee) may be contested, but the special characteristic of a tax is that it is unrelated to any specific benefit provided by the state, while a charge, or fee, is a payment for receiving some identifiable benefit. A stewardship fee is a charge for the right, conferred by the state on the steward, to use a specific plot of land or an aspect of the environment for a defined length of time. Although part of the revenue from stewardship fees

50

may provide income for the state, the rest is distributed as a Universal Income.

Most importantly, the term 'stewardship' emphasises that stewardship fees are more than just a different way of raising revenue. They represent an entirely different property system – private property without private ownership.

Stewardship support payment

When a plot of land is offered at auction it may not attract any positive bids, perhaps because the planning obligations mean that it is not profitable, for example, an urban park or wilderness area. In this case potential stewards can bid for a subsidy, a negative stewardship fee or 'stewardship support payment', and the lowest such bid secures the stewardship of the site.

Stewardship Trust

A body in a stewardship economy that acts as overall steward for some aspect of the natural world (for example, land, roads, atmosphere, oceans, watersheds, subsoil). It is responsible for managing its aspect of the natural world and allocating manageable amounts (for example, plots of land, emissions permits) to the end users.

Supply Side policies

Policies designed to intervene in the economy by influencing supply (rather than demand) to stimulate production. These include policies such as wage flexibility for the poor, i.e. encouraging people to accept low wages to 'price themselves into jobs'.

Sustainable Development

Development that meets the needs of the present without compromising the ability of future generations to meet their own needs. (United Nations p15)[48]

Sustainable development

Sustainable development is 'development that meets the needs of the present without compromising the ability of future generations

---

[48] United Nations (1987) Report of the World Commission on Environment and Development

to meet their own needs' (World Commission for Development and Environment of the United Nations 1987).

If we are interested in, say, the build-up of pollution or the depletion of natural resources we have to ask how the economy allocates resources over the course of time - we have to concern ourselves with intertemporal allocative efficiency and intertemporal equity.

Intergenerational allocative efficiency can be defined as the situation in which 'it is not possible to increase the utility of a particular household in a particular period except at the cost of decreasing the utility of that household in some other period or decreasing the utility of some other household or households in any period' (Michael Common 1996:222) .

The conditions under which the market might be capable of ensuring intertemporal allocative efficiency include all those assumptions already considered for a single time period and some others as well. For example, the information requirement is that the implications of present decisions for future production and utility is fully known in the present.

System

A system is something that can be thought of as a whole and as a set of interconnected parts.

Tax

A payment compulsorily collected from individuals or firms by central or local government (Oxford Dictionary of Economics)[49].

Tax shift

Transferring taxes from 'goods' to 'bads'.

Transfer payment

A payment for which nothing is provided in return – for example private gifts, national assistance benefits.

---

[49] The Penguin Dictionary of Economics (1984) Harmondsworth Penguin

True cost

The true cost of something to an individual or firm is the sum of the private costs (direct cost to them, the cost of inputs plus profit) and the external costs (costs borne by others, by society or by the environment). The true cost is called by economists the social cost.

True cost pricing

In ownership economies, prices of goods and services may fail to reflect some of the costs or benefits borne by people who are not parties to the sale – the externalities. These externalities often fall on the environment and/or society as a whole.

True cost pricing is an approach that seeks to assign a money value to these externalities (for example the cost of climate change) and to incorporate this into the price experienced by the purchaser and supplier.

Allocative efficiency is not achieved when producers shift (externalise) costs. If economic decisions were made taking into account the costs to environment and society as well as the firm itself, the prices of goods would be higher, and the quantities produced would be lower. The term 'true cost price' describes a price that reflects the true costs and benefits – to the firm, to society and to the environment. When consumers pay the true cost price, the polluter pays.

True price

The price established by true cost pricing.

Unemployment trap

A financial incentive structure, created by the marginal rates of taxation and withdrawal of benefits, that would be expected to deter people who are unemployed from seeking work.

Unimproved Land

See Land.

Universal Income

A Universal Income is a guaranteed (unconditional and automatic) income paid equally to every man, woman and child. It is unrelated to income, wealth, work (past, present or future), family unit in which the individual is living, marital status, gender, race or creed. It may or may not be supplemented by other state benefits.

In a stewardship economy stewardship fees are pooled and used for the benefit of all, either as government revenue or as a small independent income in the form of a Universal Income that is distributed to everyone.

Rather than using the term 'Citizen's Income' or 'Basic Income' in the context of stewardship, the term used in these books is Universal Income. This is in part to emphasise the universal and unconditional entitlement, rather than become bogged down in the inevitably exclusive definitions of citizenship and limitations to entitlement. It is mainly, however, because discussions about Citizen's Income and Basic Income have tended to focus on an income funded from conventional taxation, while a stewardship economy proposes a more generous income funded by some of the revenue from stewardship fees. Universal Income is not to be confused with the very different benefit in the U.K., Universal Credit.

Value

'Value' is widely used as a synonym for 'price established in the open market', and that is how it is generally used in this book. According to this usage the air, without which we cannot survive for more than a few minutes, has no value. This is known as the 'Paradox of Value', and is paradoxical because at times we use 'value' to describe a judgment not an economic calculation. Something has value, in the sense this is used in this book, only when people compete for it. Land, for example, has no 'value' even if it is a green and pleasant land if there is so much of it available that anybody can stake a claim to as much as they want.

See also Present Value.

Value map

A map that shows the variations in land or property values, where data are derived from market transactions and/or professional assessments made for taxation purposes (Tony Vickers)[50]. A

---

[50] Vickers, Tony (2009) *Visualising the landvaluescape: developing the case for Britain* www.landvaluescape.org/archives/2009/12/visualising-landvaluescape-for-britian-thesis-published.html Kingston University (PhD thesis)

cartographic or spatial representation of statistical data that reflects the value of land or buildings (Christopher Howes 1980:3 quoted in Tony Vickers 2009 p. 24)[51].

Valuing the environment

The costs of pollution are often expressed as a willingness to pay (WTP) for abatement. This is estimated by uncovering the amount that different sorts of people are willing to pay, and aggregating.

One approach to establishing the individual willingness to pay is just to ask people what it's worth to them – their stated preference. This approach is known to give rise to inaccuracies and inconsistencies. Another approach is to use the impact of pollution on land prices (market rents) to determine the amount that people actually do pay to avoid pollution. If it were possible to identify two plots of land, one polluted and the other unpolluted but otherwise identical, the annual cost of the pollution on an affected plot is equal to the difference in annual market rents between the two plots. In practice each plot of land has multiple factors influencing its market rent this approach requires the construction of a 'hedonic pricing model' in which the importance of all the possible factors that influence land values are estimated (by regression analysis) and a model produced that quantifies the impact of pollution.

Washington consensus

A term introduced in 1989 by John Williamson to describe the neoliberal programme supported by the American government, International Monetary Fund and World Bank. Its elements include the promotion of trade and foreign direct investment, limited budget deficits, reduced subsidies, tax reform, floating exchange rates, privatisation, deregulation and security of property rights.

Years purchase

The number of years required for the income from an asset to yield the purchase price.

---

[51] Vickers, Tony (2009) *Visualising the landvaluescape: developing the case for Britain* www.landvaluescape.org/archives/2009/12/visualising-landvaluescape-for-britian-thesis-published.html Kingston University (PhD thesis)

Yield

Yield is the return on investment. In simple terms the return on investment in land is equal to the ratio of market rent to market value.

Zero-sum game

A situation in which the losses sustained by those who lose equal the gains achieved by those who gain.

Section 2 Some economics explained

Supply and Demand

An economy can be thought of as a mechanism for choosing what goods (and services) to produce, how to produce them and to whom to distribute them. Orthodox economics focuses on one particular mechanism for making these choices, the market economy, which relies on money and prices to shape supply and demand. The most familiar alternative, the command and control economy, relies on the state to make these choices. This section begins by describing a gift economy, which relies on voluntary agreements, and contrasts this with a market economy.

Orthodox economics generally treats the economy as an equilibrium system rather than something dynamic and complex. The equilibrium system approach, though limited, is useful as a first approximation. This section uses this model to provide a graphical display of the concepts of supply, demand and elasticity.

Gift economy

Many of the important activities and transactions that take place between people do so in a gift economy, not in the market economy. Preparing food, cleaning, caring for children and older people, sharing tasks, and providing mutual help in a multitude of different ways are just some of the examples of activities that are of central importance to us as human beings. In the gift economy these activities are undertaken by people as people – what to feed the family with, how to prepare it and to whom the food is distributed are questions decided by negotiation and agreement. There is no separation between producer and consumer. People act because they choose to, because they have shared values and a shared understanding of their common good.

The scale on which such an economy can function is probably determined by the size of the group that is able to sustain these shared values and understandings. This might be described as a sort of community of purpose.

Fairness in a gift economy depends on the recognition of some form of reciprocity. Co-operation can because all benefit from it; it does not require. The accounting is usually informal, though there may be a formal accounting for gifts, including gifts of time (Edgar Cahn https://timebanks.org/)

Gift economies are fundamentally different from market economies. Goods and services are gifted within a community in which it is expected that 'what goes around comes around'. Family life, caring, spiritual practice, volunteering, some aspects of the scientific approach like peer review and most artistic creativity all take place in their own gift economies (Lewis Hyde 1979/2006:287).

Lewis Hyde describes how a gift economy establishes bonds of obligation that create a community. He also describes how people need to behave to sustain a gift economy and its community – in particular, not to hold on to or hoard a gift but make an equivalent or superior gift to others. In a gift economy people who are recognised as wealthy and powerful are those who give the greatest gifts, not those who hold on to the greatest amount of wealth. The beneficiary of a gift becomes not its owner, but its trustee (Lewis Hyde 1979/2006:15).

Gift economies seem to flourish particularly where there is common access to land and the natural world, and to be difficult to sustain in ownership economies where we receive the wealth of the natural world not as a gift but as a commodity. Lewis Hyde describes how many tribal societies understand what they take from the natural world to be a gift and treat it in a way that is appropriate to gifts – by sharing with others and by returning part of the gift to the natural world in ceremony (Lewis Hyde 1979/2006:18).

One of the features of gift economies is that gifts circulate and increase as they do so. The increase is physical where they are living organisms, social where they create community and spiritual when even inanimate gift objects are associated with increasing spiritual worth.

It is possible to think of stewardship as no more than a variation on the theme of the market economy, in which the stewardship fees are an obligation whose price is determined in the market and where people expect their Universal Income as a right. But in a stewardship economy land and natural resources are treated not as commodities to be owned and exchanged in the market but as gifts that the steward takes into their possession for a time and passes on to the next steward in due course. It is possible to think of the stewardship fees, the market rent, as the increase in the gift which then is passed on to the community. If the gift of Universal Income is then treated as a gift not a right or a commodity, some people might be able to use it to express their own gift – for example of creativity or caring – or to pass on as a gift to others or to the planet (Lewis Hyde 1979/2006:19). Stewardship could then be seen as an 'institution for the conversion of market wealth into gift wealth' (Lewis Hyde 1979/2006:283).

So, you could think of stewardship as a bridge between the worlds of gift and market economy that could provide us with a way to rediscover the energy and abundance of gift economies.

Market economy

Is it possible for co-operation to occur amongst larger groups of people, who do not necessarily share many of the same beliefs and values, without coercion and without relying on altruism? One approach is the market mechanism, which uses the price mechanism to provide answers to the same questions – what to produce, how to produce it and to whom to distribute it. A market is a mechanism by which buyers and sellers of a commodity interact to determine its price and the quantity that is made available.

The circular flow model

The way in which the price mechanism directs the economy is often described using the circular flow model (Fig 1). This simple version of the model does not include imports, exports, savings and investment.

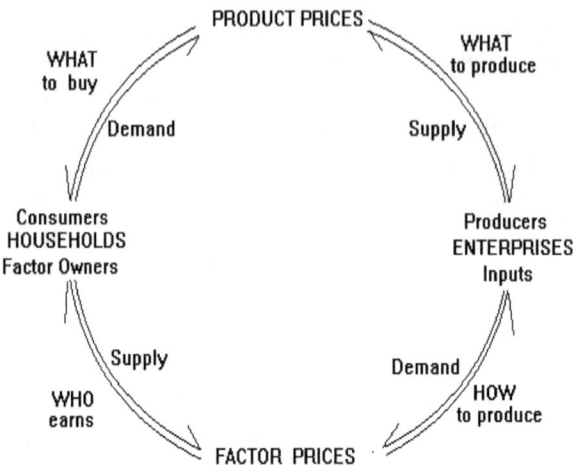

Figure 1 The Circular Flow Model

In the top arm of the model the prices of products (goods and services) are determined by the interaction of the demand of households (consumers who want the goods and services) with the supply of enterprises (firms who want to sell them). The price itself then informs households how much of each good they can purchase and informs producers how much they should produce.

In the bottom arm of the model the prices of the factors of production (land, labour and capital) are determined by the interaction of the demand of enterprises for the factors with the supply of households who provide the factors. These prices then inform enterprises how much of each factor they can purchase and inform households how much of each factor they should make available.

Market equilibrium

Nineteenth century physics made use of models based on the mathematics of its time, approximating non-linear relationships with linear equations and complex dynamic behaviour with models of equilibrium, stasis, exponential growth or periodic oscillations. Classical economics made use of similar mathematical and modelling techniques to describe the functioning of a market economy - one of the most complete examples of which was the Walrasian general equilibrium model.

Just as in physics, this approach to simplifying the complexity of real life led to great advances in our understanding and ability to predict and control the world. Just as in physics, the models are only valid under rather limited conditions. In the last 25 years economics has been transformed by incorporating more realistic assumptions about incomplete information and imperfect markets. And the discipline of complexity and non-linear systems is leading to new insights into the dynamics not just of physics but of the way the economy functions (Eric Beinhocker 2005).

In spite of the limitations of the equilibrium model, it does illuminate the way in which parts of the system work over short periods of time. It provides a way of exploring how taxation might affect economic behaviour.

Demand

The amount of a good that people are prepared to buy at any particular price is called the 'demand' for that good. It depends both on how much they want it and on how much money they have to turn this want into an actual purchase. For most categories of goods, when its price is high demand is low - the 'demand curve' shows a downward-sloping curve (Figure 2).

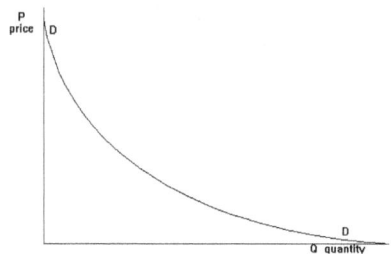

Figure 2 Demand curve

Supply

For most goods, if the price rises then producers will be encouraged to produce more, and new producers are tempted into the market. The supply curve will tend to be upward sloping (Figure 3).

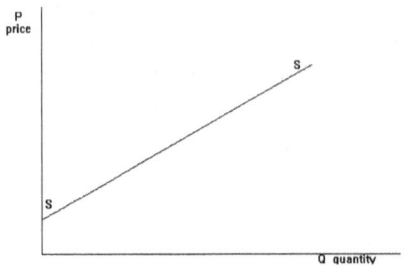

Figure 3 Supply curve

Equilibrium price

The equilibrium market model suggests that where there is a free market, price and quantity will be determined by the intersection of the curves for supply and demand. Suppliers are satisfied anywhere on the supply curve; consumers are satisfied anywhere on the demand curve and both are satisfied at the point of equilibrium E (Figure.4). For example, if prices rise above this point, producers will respond by supplying more while demand will fall. In the relative glut that follows, prices will fall back towards the equilibrium. Similar self-correcting mechanisms come into play for any change in P or Q. As with any negative feedback mechanism, if delays or partial information are introduced this 'self-correcting' mechanism may oscillate.

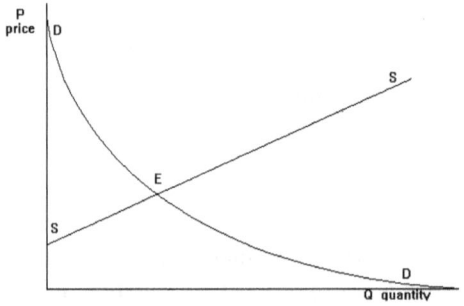

Figure 4 Equilibrium

Marginal Utility

The level of demand for a particular good will depend on how much satisfaction people get from it as well as on their level of disposable income/wealth. The second unit of ice-cream gives less satisfaction than the first (the empirical 'law of diminishing (marginal) returns'), so a plot of satisfaction (utility) against quantity gives a curve that flattens off with increasing amounts (Figure 5).

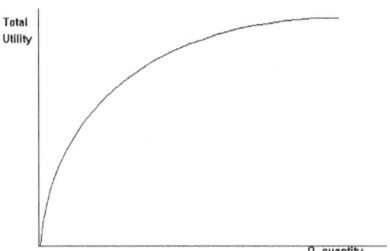

Figure 5 Utility curve

Another way of representing this is as a plot of **marginal utility**, the increase in utility that occurs as result of the last unit consumed. This curve, which is equal to the slope of the utility curve, is downward sloping (Figure 6).

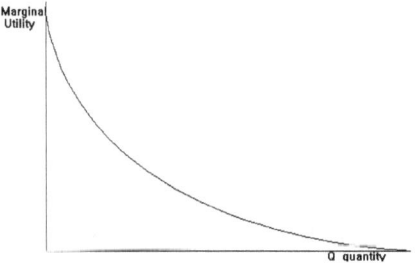

Figure 6 Marginal Utility curve

Adam Smith (1776 Volume I Book I Chapter IV:41) articulated the 'paradox of value': commodities that are essential to life like water (which have a high value in use) may have a low value in exchange (price), while commodities that are inessential like non-industrial diamonds (which have a low value in use) may have a high value in exchange (price). Demand, and thus price, is determined not by *total* utility but by *marginal* utility – not by the average satisfaction derived from all the glasses of water we purchase, but by the satisfaction derived from the last glass purchased.

The price established in a market may be very different from its value in use, although the terms are often used as though they mean the same thing, and in an economic system people frequently treat them as the same.

Elasticity

The general shape of the supply and demand curves can be described by their elasticity. The price elasticity of supply is the percentage change in the amount supplied for a unit percentage change in price. The price elasticity of demand is the percentage change in the amount demanded for a unit percentage change in price.

The supply and demand curves when elasticity = 1 (unit elasticity) are shown below (Figures 7 and 8). The shapes of these curves (upward sloping supply and downward sloping demand) are those we have so far considered.

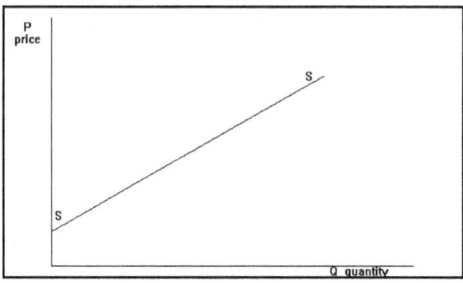

Figure 7 Supply curve, unit elasticity

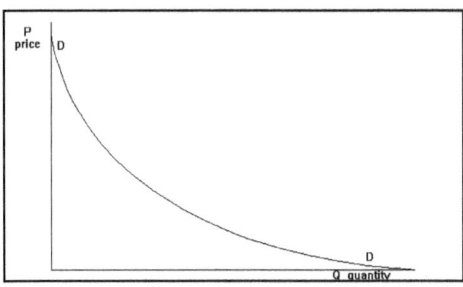

Figure 8 Demand curve, unit elasticity

When supply is perfectly elastic it requires only a small increase in the price of goods to produce an infinitely large increase in supply. An example would be goods whose industrial production can be readily increased as all the inputs are readily available (Figure 9).

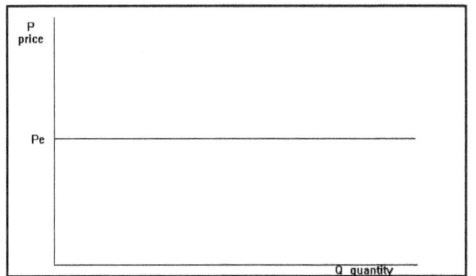

Figure 9   Perfectly elastic supply

Where supply is perfectly inelastic the quantity supplied cannot be increased no matter what price is offered. An example would be a painting by Leonardo da Vinci. It is usually argued that land is inelastic in supply as its amount is fixed and it cannot be created or destroyed (Figure 10).

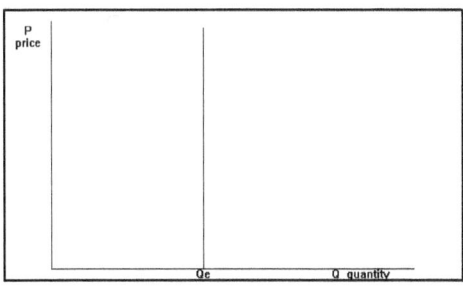

Figure 10 Perfectly inelastic supply

Rent

The concepts at the heart of the efficiency arguments of this book –
the economic surplus, rent, and market rent - are illustrated here.

When supply and demand have unit elasticity

Where demand and supply are in equilibrium at E, the quantity
produced is Qe at a price Pe (Figure 11) . Demand reflects marginal
utility, the slope of the demand curve, so the *total utility* is
proportional to the *area* under the demand curve. The total utility of
a quantity Qe is the area under the demand curve up to this quantity
(shaded area in the figure).

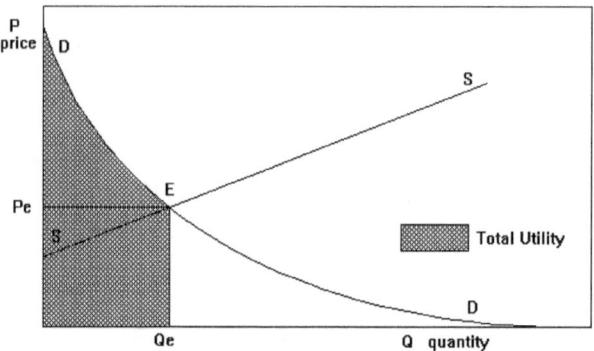

Figure 11

The supply curve reflects the marginal costs of producing the goods
and the area under the supply curve is the total cost of producing the
goods. Total production costs of a quantity Qe are shown as the
shaded area below (Fig.12).

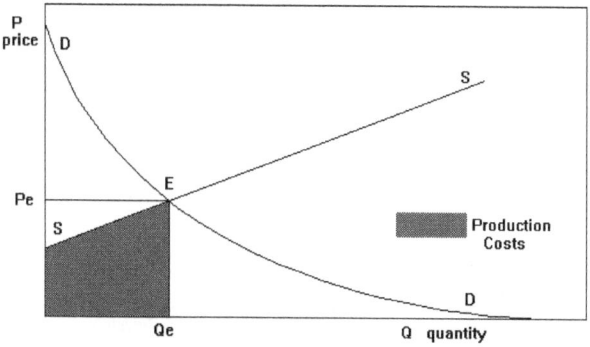

Figure 12

The difference between the total utility of goods and the cost of producing them is referred to as the **economic surplus** (Fig. 13).

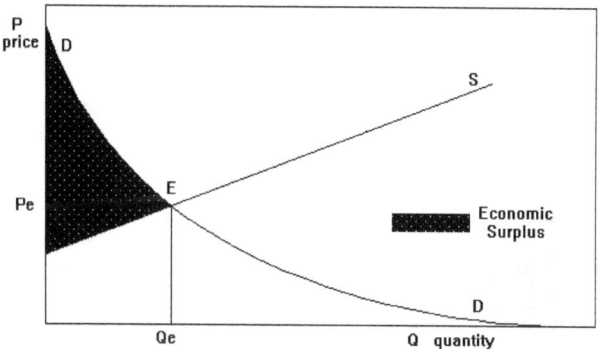

Figure 13

The economic surplus can be divided into two parts by the line PeE (Fig. 14). The area below this line but above the supply curve represents goods sold at a market price that is greater than the cost of production and is referred to as the **producer surplus** – the difference between what the producer receives and the amount that they would have been prepared to sell for. The area of economic surplus above the line but below the demand curve represents goods bought at a market price that is less than their marginal utility and is referred to as the **consumer surplus** - the difference between what the consumer actually pays and what they would have been prepared to pay. The consumer surplus only exists when the demand curve is downward-sloping.

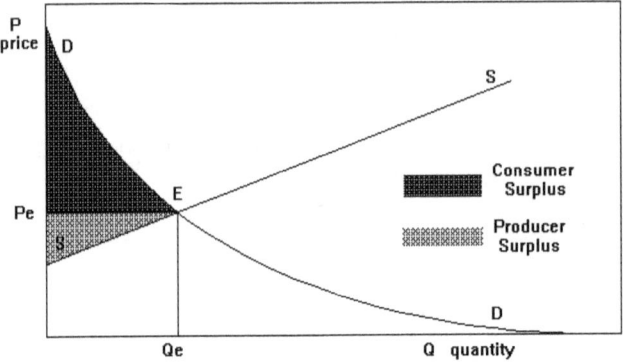

Figure 14

When supply is perfectly elastic

If you imagine the slope of the supply curve (Fig. 14) decreasing till it is zero, supply is perfectly elastic (Fig. 15).

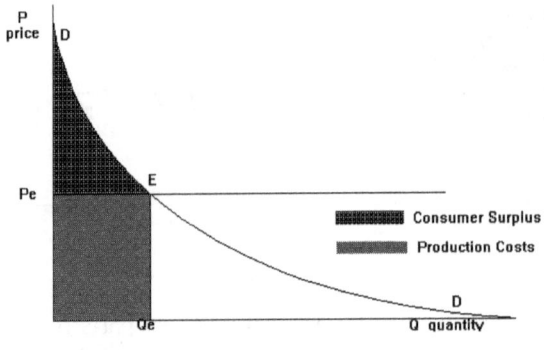

Figure 15

As this occurs, the size of the producer surplus falls until it disappears when supply is perfectly elastic.

This is the long-term position in a market where there is perfect competition. All firms are price-takers – that is, they accept market prices which they cannot influence by monopoly powers (e.g., size, patents, niche markets, ownership of important land sites). They

68

compete by cutting prices to the level where only production costs are covered.

When supply is perfectly inelastic (fixed)

If, by contrast, you imagine the slope of the supply curve increasing till it is vertical, supply is perfectly inelastic (Fig. 16).

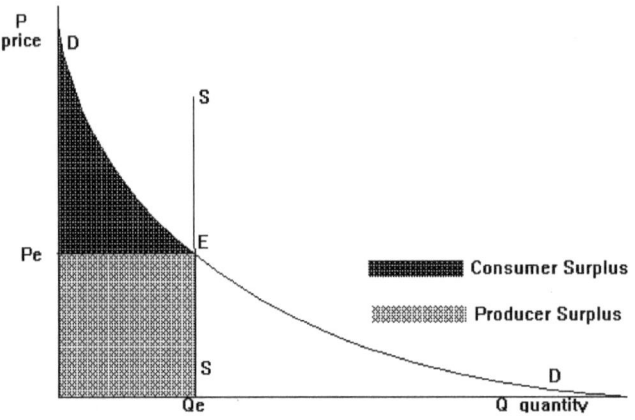

Figure 16

Here, for example the painting by Leonardo da Vinci, the quantity supplied is unaffected by the price offered. There are no costs of production, and the producer surplus accrues to the current supplier not to the original producer.

Rent

The term 'pure economic rent', or sometimes just 'rent', is applied by economists to payment for any factor that is fixed in supply.

Rare paintings are peripheral to the bulk of economic activity. However, land is a universally important economic factor that is virtually fixed in supply. In this book, payments for land and natural resources are referred to as 'rent' while payments for things made by people but fixed in supply (Leonardo's painting) are not.

Let us consider the rent of unimproved land, looking again at figure 16.

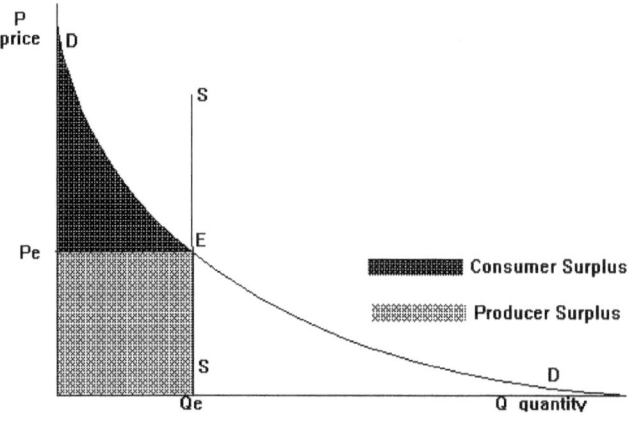

Figure 16

The quantity of land is Qe and the current demand curve is DD (Fig. 16). The current equilibrium rent of land is Pe. When land is leased at this price the land-user benefits from the consumer surplus. There are no production costs. The landowner benefits from the whole of the producer surplus – the rent.

The Deadweight loss: Effect of Taxation on Production

This section uses supply and demand curves to explore the effect of taxation on production. It uses examples of taxing both inputs to production (the factors of production in the lower arm of the circular flow model) and outputs of production (the goods and services in the upper arm of the circular flow model).

The graphical display of the consumer and producer surplus is used to illustrate the deadweight loss of conventional taxation.

Supply and demand have unit elasticity

Suppose that a tax is introduced on an output, which may be goods or services. Before the tax is introduced, a quantity Qe is purchased at a price Pe. After the tax is introduced the quantity produced falls from Qe to Qe' and the price received by the provider falls from Pe to Pe'. The gross price paid by the consumer however rises from Pe to Pe'+T (Fig. 17).

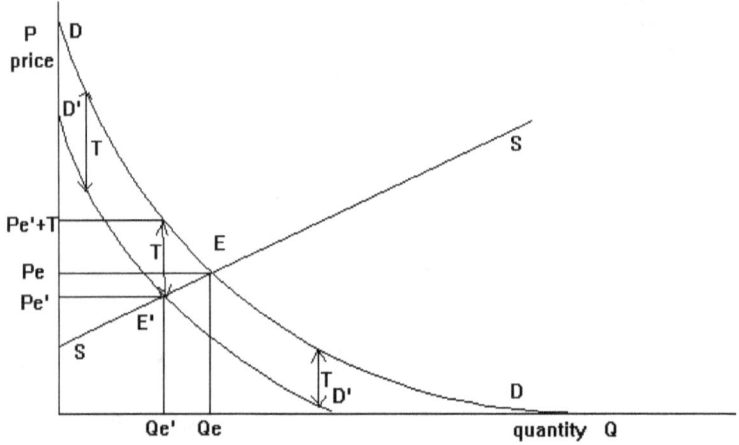

Figure 17

That is to say, the demand curve is displaced downwards by an amount equal to the tax T, from the curve DD to D'D'.

The consumer and producer surplus before taxation is shown in Fig. 18 below.

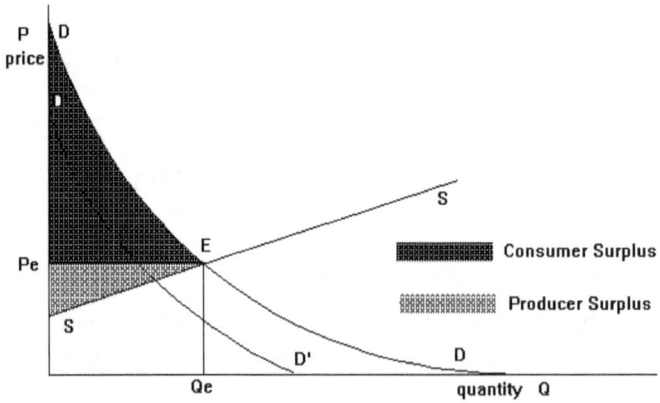

Figure 18

After taxation the consumer and producer surplus are both reduced Part of the reason for this is that some of the economic surplus has been captured as tax (the government surplus).

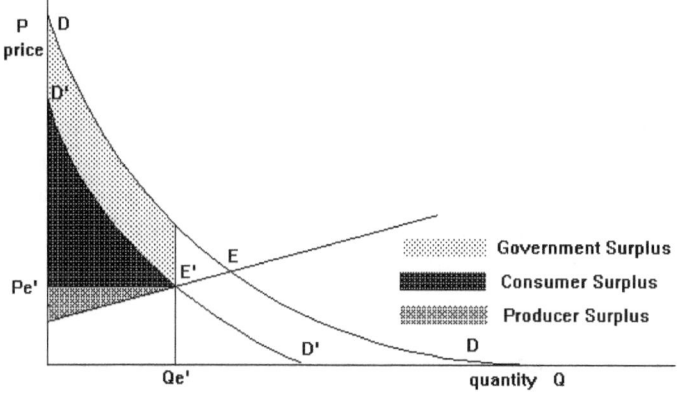

Figure 19

There is also a reduction of the total economic surplus due to the reduced quantity supplied (Qe'). This lost surplus is shown below (Fig. 20).

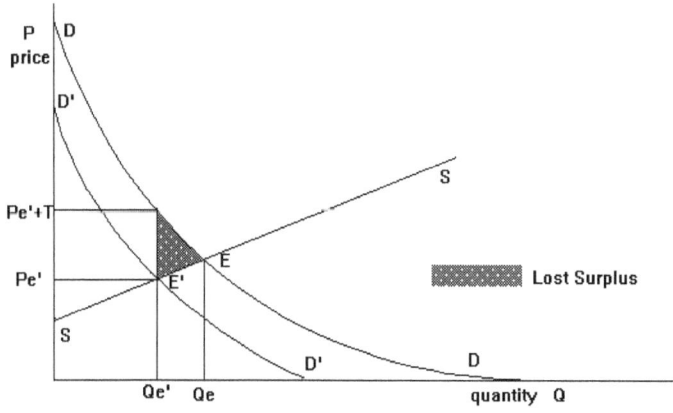

Figure 20

This lost surplus comprises losses in both the consumer surplus and the producer surplus. It is a measure of the inefficiency of taxation, its disincentive effect on production, the 'deadweight loss of taxation'. The extent of this loss depends on the elasticity of both supply and demand.

Supply or demand are perfectly inelastic

Taxation of an input or output for which supply or demand is inelastic is an example of a **Ramsey tax**. Frank Ramsey identified the most efficient kinds of tax and the term 'Ramsey tax' is applied to a tax that has no impact on the quantity of production or consumption of the good being taxed. It therefore does not cause any loss of the economic surplus and not distort the allocative efficiency of the market.

Inelastic demand

Where demand is perfectly inelastic, the consumer will, if necessary, pay any price at all to purchase the output. An example is a poll tax, though here it is in reality a matter of conforming with the law rather than making a purchase. A poll tax is efficient (but it is also unjust).

Inelastic supply

With a perfectly inelastic supply there are no production costs (Fig. 21). The producer surplus arises because the supply cannot be expanded.

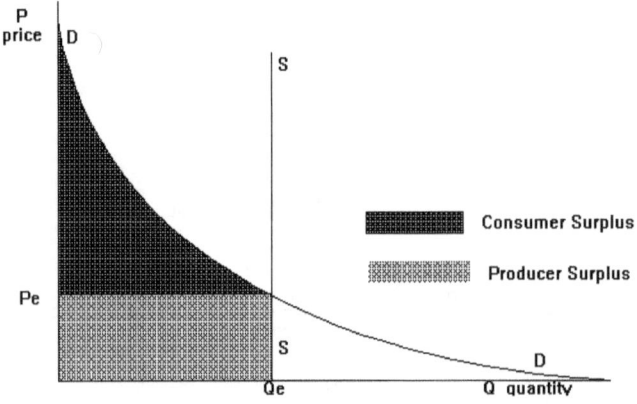

Figure 21

I

In this situation a tax (the government surplus) eats into the producer surplus. Critically, there is no lost surplus (Fig. 22).

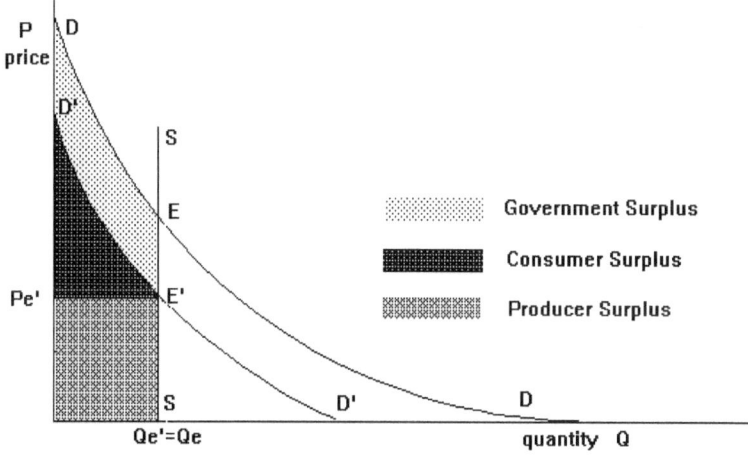

Figure 22

Section 3 Bibliography and links

All links accessed 2021.

Acioli, Claudio 'The challenge of slum formation in the developing world', *Land Lines*, 19.2, (2007), 2-7.

Alaska Permanent Fund Corporation. https://apfc.org/

Alyea, Paul Edgar, and Blanche R. Alyea. 1956. *Fairhope, 1894-1954; the story of a single tax colony* (University of Alabama Press: University, Ala.).

Andelson, Robert (ed). 2000. Land value taxation around the world (Oxford:Blackwells).

Aquinas, St Thomas Summa Theologica.2000. (Ave Maria Press: Notre Dame In.).

AREIS (Auditors Real Estate Information System) AREIS property information search http://co.lucas.oh.us/index.aspx?NID=377

Aristotle, *Politics Bk 2*, trans. by Benjamin Jowett 350 BCE http://classics.mit.edu/Aristotle/politics.2.two.html

Arnott, R., Petrova, P. The Property Tax as a Tax on Value: Deadweight Loss. *Int Tax Public Finan* 13, (2006), 241–266 https://doi.org/10.1007/s10797-006-4938-6

Arthur, W. Brian. 2014. *Complexity and the Economy* (Oxford University Press: New York).

Atkinson, Dan, Elliott, Larry. 2008. *The gods that failed : how blind faith in markets has cost us our future* (Bodley Head: London).

Auerbach, Alan J., and Martin S. Feldstein. 2002. *Handbook of public economics* (Elsevier: Amsterdam).

Axelrod, Robert M. 1984. *The evolution of cooperation* (Basic Books: New York).

Ballard, Charles L, Shoven, John B. & Whalley, John, 'General equilibrium computations of the marginal welfare costs of taxes in the United States', *American Economic Review*, 75, (1985a), 128-138.

Ballard, Charles L., Shoven, John B. & Whalley, John. 'The Total Welfare Cost of the United States Tax System: A General Equilibrium Approach', *National Tax Journal*, 38, (1985b),125-40.

Banks, Ronald. 1989. *Costing the earth* (London: Shepheard-Walwyn).

Barker, Kate. 2004. *Delivering stability: securing our future housing needs* (Norwich: HMSO)   http://www.andywightman.com/docs/barker_housing_final.pdf

Barlow, James. 2002. *Land for housing: current practice and future options* (published for the Joseph Rowntree Foundation by YPS: York).

Barnes, Peter. 2001. *Who owns the sky? : our common assets and the future of capitalism* (Island Press: Washington, DC).

Basic Income Grant Coalition. 2009. *Making the difference! The BIG in Namibia.*   www.bignam.org/Publications/BIG_Assessment_report_08b.pdf

BasicIncome.org   www.basicincome.org/news/2017/10/overview-of-current-basic-income-related-experiments-october-2017/.

Bateman, John. 1873 and 1879. *The great landowners of Great Britain and Ireland* (Harrison: London).

Beckwith, Martha. 1940/1970. *Hawaiian mythology* (University of Hawaii Press: Hawaii).

Beinhocker, Eric D. 2006. *The origin of wealth : evolution, complexity, and the radical remaking of economics* (Harvard Business School Press: Boston, Mass.).

Bentham, J 1838-1843 Principles of the civil code: *The Works of Jeremy Bentham,* published under the Superintendence of his Executor, John Bowring (William Tait: Edinburgh) 311-2.

Black, Douglas Sir, Townsend, Peter and Davidson, Nick. 1980. *Inequalities in health: the Black report* (Penguin, 1982: Harmondsworth).

Blanc, Louis (1850 (9th edn)) *Organisation du travail* (Nouveau Montopolis)

Boles, Nicholas. 'It sounds bonkers but we should embrace a land tax', *Financial Times,* 29 September 2011.

Blumenfeld, Samuel. 1974. *Property in a Humane Economy: A Selection of Essays.* (Open Court Publishing: Chicago).

Bordo, Michael & Jeanne, Olivier. 'Boom-busts in asset prices, economic instability & monetary policy.' *CEPR working paper 3398* May 2002.

Brand, Stewart. 1994. *How buildings learn : what happens after they're built* (Viking: New York, NY).

Braund, Mark, 'Land Value Taxation: a genuine alternative', *Guardian,* 25 September 2010.

Burke, Eleanor, Burke, Simon & Christidis, Nikolaos. 'Modeling the recent evolution of global drought and projections for the twenty-first century with the Hadley Centre climate model' *Journal of Hydrometerology* 7:5 (2006) 1113-1125.

Burnham, Andy, 'Land Value Taxation – not old or New but true Labour', *Guardian,* 26 August 2010.

Burtraw, Dallas. 2000. 'Innovation Under the Tradable Sulphur Dioxide Emission Permits Program in the US Electricity Sector' *OECD Workshop On Innovation and the Environment* 19 June 2000.

Cahill, Kevin. 2001. *Who owns Britain* (Canongate: Edinburgh).

Campbell, Joseph, and Bill D. Moyers. 1988. *The power of myth* (Doubleday: New York).

Caporaso, James A., and David P. Levine. 1992. *Theories of political economy* (Cambridge University Press: Cambridge, New York).

Capra, Fritjof. 1996. *The web of life : a new scientific understanding of living systems* (Anchor Books: New York).

Caravanpriceguide.com link no longer available

Carter, Alan. 1989. *The philosophical foundations of property rights* (Harvester, Wheatsheaf: New York ; London).

Chapman, John 'The extent and nature of agricultural enclosure.'

Agricultural History Review 35:1 (1987) 25-35.

Cheshire, Paul & Sheppard, Stephen C. 'Capitalising the Value of Free Schools: The Impact of Supply Constraints and Uncertainty.' *The Economic Journal* 114(499) (2004) 397-397.

Cicero. *De finibus* quoted in Tully 1980. 71.

Cicero, M. T., & Miller, W. (1928). *Cicero De officiis*. (Heinemann: London).

Cicero: *De Re Publica* ed. J. E. G. Zetzel (54-54BC/1995) (Cambridge University Press: Cambridge, U.K.).

Citizen's Basic Income Trust   What is Universal Basic Income? 2021
https://citizensincome.org/citizens-income/what-is-it/

Citizen's Income Trust   Newsletter Issue 1   p. 3. 2008
https://citizensincome.org/wp-content/uploads/2016/02/CIT_Newsletter_2008_Issue_1.pdf

Coalition for Economic Justice *Reform of Business Rates*. 2013
www.c4ej.com/cej-publications/reform-of-business-rates

Coase, Ronald. 'The Federal Communications Commission'. *Journal of Law and Economics* 2 (1959) 1-40.

Collier, Paul, Hoeffler, Anke. 'Greed and Grievance in Civil War.' *Policy Research Working Paper* 2355. (World Bank, Washington, DC).

Common, Michael. 1988/1996. *Environmental and resource economics.* (Longman: Harlow).

Conaty, Pat, Birchall, Johnston, Bendle, Steve & Foggitt, Rosemary. 2003. *Common ground - for mutual home ownership* (New Economics Foundation: London).

Connelan, Owen Valuation of specialised Public Sector Assets. *Property Management* 15:4 (1997).

Conway, Moncure. 1894. The writings of Thomas Paine (Putnam's Sons: New York).

Crafts, Nicholas & Leunig, Timothy. 2006. *The historical significance of transport for economic growth and productivity* (London School of Economics: London).
80

Crowley, Robert. 1547. *An information and petition against the oppressors of the poor commons of this realm: an address to parliament.*

Dasgupta, Partha. 2001. *Human well-being and the natural environment* (Oxford University Press: Oxford).

Davis, Morris A, Heathcote, Jonathan. 2004. 'The price and quantity of residential land in the United States.' *Finance and Economics Discussion Series* 2004-37, Board of Governors of the Federal Reserve System (U.S.). www.federalreserve.gov/pubs/feds/2004/200437/200437abs.html

de Bruyn, Sander et al. 2016. *Calculation of additional profits of sectors and firms from the EU ETS* (CE Delft: Delft) https://cedelft.eu/wp-content/uploads/sites/2/2021/03/CE_Delft_7K42_Calculation_additional_profits_EU_ETS_FINAL.pdf

de Soto, Hernando. 2000/2001. *The mystery of capital: why capitalism triumphs in the west and fails everywhere else.* (Black: London).

Denman, D. R. 1984. *Markets under the sea?: a study of the potential of private property rights in the seabed* (Institute of Economic Affairs: London).

Dennys, Nick. *Land and Liberty* Summer 14 2002.

Department for Communities and Local Government. Homes for the future: more affordable, more sustainable. (Department of Communities and Local Government: London, 2007).

Department for Communities and Local Government. Place matters: the location strategy for the United Kingdom. (Department for Communities and Local Government: London, 2008).

Department for Communities and Local Government. Draft National Planning Policy Framework. (Department for Communities and Local Government: London, 2009).

Department for the Environment, Food & Rural affairs. An introductory guide to valuing ecosystem services. (Department for the Environment, Food & Rural affairs: London, 2007).

Department for Transport. Transport Analysis Guidance. (Department for Transport: London, 2012).

Department for Work and Pensions. Income-related benefits: Estimates of Take-up 2016/17 (Department for Work and Pensions: London, 2018) https://assets.publishing.service.gov.uk/government/uploads/system/uploads/attachment_data/file/757268/income-related-benefits-estimates-of-take-up-2016-17.pdf 1-2.

Department for Work and Pensions. Resource accounts 2008-9 (Department for Work and Pensions: London, 2010) 44,66.

Department of the Environment. Second Interim Evaluation of Enterprise Zones. (Department of the Environment: London, 1988).

Diamond, Jared. 1997. *Guns, germs and steel : a short history of everybody for the last 13,000 years* (Vintage, 2005: London).

Diamond, Jared. 2005. *Collapse : how societies choose to fail or survive* (Allen Lane: London).

Dollar, David & Pritchett, Lant. 1998. *Assessing aid: what works, what doesn't, and why* (Oxford University Press: New York) https://documents1.worldbank.org/curated/en/612481468764422935/pdf/multi-page.pdf

Dorfman, Robert; Samuelson, Paul; Solow, Robert M. 1958. *Linear programming and economic analysis.* (McGraw-Hill: New York).

Dorling, Danny. 2010. *Injustice : why social inequality persists* (Policy: Bristol).

Dorling, Danny. 2011. Talk at Dartington Hall, Totnes, Devon.

Douglas, Clifford Hugh. 1924. *Social Credit* (Cecil Palmer: London).

Dryden, John Works translated by Dryden. 1697. *The Works of Virgil: containing his Pastorals, Georgics, and Æneis. Translated into English verse; by Mr Dryden. (The life of P. V. M.) L.P* (London).

Dworkin, Ronald. 1979/1992. *Taking rights seriously.* (Duckworth: London).

Dye, Richard F., Richard W. England, and Lincoln Institute of Land Policy. 2009. *Land value taxation : theory, evidence, and practice* (Lincoln Institute of Land Policy: Cambridge, Mass.)

Dyson, Ben et al. 2011. Submission to the Independent Commission on Banking. (Positive Money: London) https://positivemoney.org/wp-content/uploads/2010/11/NEF-Southampton-Positive-Money-ICB-Submission.pdf

82

Economist The 9/12/95; 5/11/97; 28/2/98; 21/11/98; 24/7/2004; 13/05/06; 23/9/06; 9/11/06; 10/3/07; 17/3/07; 4/2/12; 9/6/12; 29/6/13; 24/4/14: 23/8/14; 20/9/14; 17/1/15; 4/6/16; 5/11/16; 19/8/18)

Eddington, Rod. 2006. *The Eddington transport study : main report: transport's role in sustaining the UK's productivity and competitiveness.* (Stationery Office: Norwich).

Eisenstein, Charles. 2011. *Sacred economics : money, gift, & society in the age of transition* (Evolver Editions: Berkeley, Calif.).

Ekins, Paul. 1993. *Trading off the future : making world trade environmentally sustainable* (New Economics Foundation).

Elliott, Larry, 'Take on the City with a 'people's budget', *Guardian,* Business, 22 March 2010.

Elliott, Larry, Atkinson, Dan. 2008. *The gods that failed : how blind faith in markets has cost us our future* (Bodley Head: London).

Emeny, Roger & Wilks, Hector. 1984. *Principles and practice of rating valuation.* 4th edition.(The Estates Gazette: London).

EUROMOD https://www.euromod.ac.uk/

European Union. 2007. Inspire Directive. https://inspire.ec.europa.eu/about-inspire/563

Evans, David B. 2004. *Copenhagen Consensus: Comments on the Challenge Paper on Communicable Diseases* (World Health Organization: Geneva) 14 September 2004.

Ewald Engelen, Ismail Ertürk, Julie Froud, Sukhdev Johal, Adam Leaver, Mick Moran, Adriana Nilsson, and Karel Williams. 2011. *After the Great Complacence: Financial Crisis and the Politics of Reform* (Oxford University Press: Oxford) 47.

Feeny, David. Birkes, Fikret, McCay Bonnie J, Acheson, James M, 'The Tragedy of the Commons: Twenty-Two Years Later' *Human Ecology*, 18. 1. (1990).

Feldstein, Martin, 'Tax avoidance and the deadweight loss of the Income Tax', *Review of Economics and Statistics*, 81.4 (1999), 674-680.

Filmer, Robert. 1680. *Patriarcha, or the natural power of Kings* (Walter

Davis: London).

Fischer, Irving. 1936. *100% Money.*

Fitz Nigel Richard 1176 Dialogus de Scaccario (The Dialogue of the Exchequer).

Flanagan, Robert J. 1989. *Economics of the employment relationship* (Scott, Foresman: Glenview, Ill.; London).

Flanagan, R., Norman, G., & Meadows, J. 1989. *Life cycle costing: theory and practice* (BSP Professional Books).

Fleming, David. 2005. *Energy and the common purpose : descending the energy staircase with tradable energy quotas (TEQs)* (The Lean Economy Connection: London). https://www.flemingpolicycentre.org.uk/EnergyAndTheCommonPurpose.pdf

Foner, Eric. Purchase and/or conquest, *London Review of Books,* February 9 2006, 7-18.

Foundation for the Economics of Sustainability (FEASTA) climate and energy working group. 2006/2007. The great emissions rights give-away www.feasta.org/2007/03/11/the-great-emissions-rights-give-away/

Foundation for the Economics of Sustainability (FEASTA). 2008. Cap and share: a fair way to cut greenhouse emissions www.feasta.org/documents/energy/Cap-and-Share-May08.pdf FEASTA

Friedman, Milton. 1960. *A Program for Monetary Stability* (Fordham University Press: New York).

Froud, Julie, Johal, Sukdev, Law, John, Leaver, Adam and Williams, Karel. 2011. *Rebalancing the economy (or buyer's remorse): CRESC working* paper 87. (Centre for Research on Socio-Cultural Change: Milton Keynes).

Gaffney, Mason. 'Land as a distinctive factor of production' in Tideman, Nicolaus. 1994. *Land and taxation* (Shepheard-Walwyn in association with Centre for Incentive Taxation: London).

Galbraith, John Kenneth, Frank Moraes, and Edward Horne. 1974. *John Kenneth Galbraith introduces India* (Deutsch: London).

Galbraith, John Kenneth. 1987. *A history of economics* (Hamish Hamilton: London).
84

Galbraith, John Kenneth. 1992. *The culture of contentment* (Sinclair-Stevenson: London).

George, Henry. 1879. *Progress and poverty* (Wm M Hinton: San Francisco).

Gilder, George F. 1981. *Wealth & poverty* (Buchan & Enright, 1982: London).

Girardet, Herbert (compiler) 1976. *Land for the people* (Crescent Books: London).

Give Directly https://www.givedirectly.org/ubi-study/

Glover, Christopher 2013. How is land valued? https://www.landvaluetax.org/valuations/how-is-land-valued-sp-668440

Goodhart, Charles, 'The two concepts of money: implications for the analysis of optimal currency areas.' *European Journal of Political Economy* 14.3 (August 1998), 407-432.

Gorringe, Tim. 2002. *A theology of the built environment : justice, empowerment, redemption* (Cambridge University Press: Cambridge, U.K.).

Gov.Uk. Introduction to Business Rates www.gov.uk/introduction-to-business-rates/overview

Graves, Tommas. 2011. Debt is inevitable – unless we change our ways www.landisfree.co.uk/?p=243

National Audit, Office. 2018. *HM Treasury : PFI and PF2* (Dandy Booksellers Ltd: London).

Greater London Authority (GLA) Economics. A fairer London: the 2008 living wage in London. (Greater London Authority (GLA) Economics: London, 2008).

Grotius, Hugo. 1625. *The Laws of War and Peace.* Transl. Innys, W. & Mangy, R. 1738.

Guest, Anthony Gordon. 1961. *Oxford essays in jurisprudence* (Oxford University Press: London).

Gwartney, James & Lawson, Robert. Economic freedom of the world: 2007 annual report. (Frazer Institute: Vancouver, 2007).

Gwartney, Ted. 1999. *Estimating land values* (Robert Schalkenbach Foundation: New York)(www.henrygeorge.org/ted.htm)

Hamilton, Kirk. 2006. *Where is the wealth of nations? : measuring capital for the 21st century* (World Bank: Basingstoke; Palgrave: Washington, D.C.).

Harberger, Arnold. 1964. *Taxation, resource allocation and welfare* in National Bureau of Economic Research and the Brookings Institution, *The Role of Direct and Indirect Taxes in the Federal Reserve System* (Princeton University Press: Princeton, N.J.).

Hardin, Garrett. 'The tragedy of the commons.' *Science,* 162 (1968) 1243-8.

Hardy, Dennis. 1979. *Alternative communities in 19th century England* (Longmans: London).

Harris C L (ed) 1973. *Government spending and land values: public money and private gain Wisconsin* (University of Winconsin Press: Wisconsin).

Harrison, Fred. 1983. *The power in the land : an inquiry into unemployment, the profits crisis and land speculation* (Shepheard-Walwyn: London).

Harrison, Fred. 1998. *The losses of nations : deadweight politics versus public rent dividends* (Othila: London).

Harrison, Fred. 2005. *Boom Bust: House prices, banking and the depression of 2100* (Shepheard-Walwyn: London).

Harrison, Fred. 2006a. *Wheels of fortune* (Institute of Economic Affairs: London).

Harrison, Fred. 2006b. *Ricardo's Law: house prices and the great tax clawback scam* (Shepheard-Walwyn: London).

Harrison, Fred. 2008. *The silver bullet* (The International Union for Land Value Taxation: London).

Harrison, Fred, and Mason, Gaffney. 2016. *Rent unmasked: how to save the global economy and build a sustainable future: essays in honour of Mason Gaffney* (Shepheard-Walwyn: London).

Hart, Keith. 1982. *The political economy of West African agriculture.* (Cambridge University Press: Cambridge).

Hartwick, John M., and John M. Hartwick. 1977. *Intergenerational equity and the investment of rents from exhaustible resources in a two sector model and Notes on the economics of forestry exploitation* (Institute for Economic Research, Queen's University: Kingston, Ont.).

Hartzog, Alanna, 'Pennsylvania's success with local property tax reform: the split rate tax.' *American Journal of Economics and Sociology* (April 1997) reprinted in Hartzog, Alanna (2008) *The earth belongs to everyone* (Institute for Economic Democracy: Radford VA).

Hartzog, Alanna. 2008.*The earth belongs to everyone* (Institute for Economic Democracy: Radford VA).

Heinberg, Richard. 2003. *The party's over: oil, war and the fate of industrial societies* (New Society Publishers: Gabriola, BC).

Herring, Richard & , and Susan M. Wachter. 1999. *Real estate booms and banking busts: an international perspective* (Group of Thirty: Washington, D.C.).

Hill, Christopher. 1972. *The world turned upside down : radical ideas during the English revolution* (Penguin, 1991: London).

HM Revenue and Customs. 2018. Child Benefit, Child Tax Credit and Working Tax Credit Take-up rates 2016. https://assets.publishing.service.gov.uk/government/uploads/system/uploads/attachment_data/file/851148/Child_Benefit__Child_Tax_Credit_and_Working_Tax_Credit_take-up_rates_2016_to_2017_restated.pdf p.6

HM Treasury, Budget 2005: Financial statement and budget report. (HM Treasury: London, 2005).

HM Treasury The green book: appraisal and evaluation in central government. (HM Treasury: London, 2007).

Hobbes, Thomas. 1649. *Elementa philosophica de eigenelements' philosophiques du citoyen. Traicte\0301 politique, ou\0300 les fondemens de la Societe\0301 civile sont descouverts ... Traduicts en Franc\0327ois par un de ses amis. The translator's dedicatory epistle signed: Sorbiere.* (Iean Blaeu: Amsterdam).

Hodgkinson, Brian. 2008. *A new model of the economy* (Shepheard-Walwyn in association with The School of Economic Science: London).

Honoré, A. M. 1961. 'Ownership.' In Guest, Anthony Gordon. *Oxford essays in jurisprudence* (Oxford University Press: London, 1961) 107–147.

Hopkins, A.G. 1973. *An economic history of West Africa* (Longman: London).

Hopkins, Rob. 2009. *The transition handbook : from oil dependency to local resilience* (Green Books: Totnes, Devon).

House of Commons Treasury Committee: Independent Commission on Banking 2011 https://publications.parliament.uk/pa/cm201012/cmselect/cmtreasy/1069/1069.pdf

House of Commons Work and Pensions Committee 2007a) Benefits simplification HC 463 (The Stationery Office: Norwich).

House of Commons Work and Pensions Committee 2007b) Benefits simplification: government response HC1054 (The Stationery Office: Norwich).

Huber, Joseph, and James Robertson. 2000. *Creating new money : a monetary reform for the information age* (New Economics Foundation: London).

Hudson, Michael. 2000. 'Mesopotamia and Classical Antiquity.' in Andelson, Robert (ed). 2000. Land value taxation around the world (Oxford:Blackwells).

Hueting, Roefie, Bosch, Peter and de Boer, Bart. 1992. *Methodology for calculation of sustainable national income* (International Union for Conservation of Nature: Gland, Switzerland).

Hume, David. 1902 (1936) *Enquiries concerning the Human Understanding and Concerning the Principles of Morals* (Clarendon Press: Oxford).

Huntingdon, Charles White. 1922. *Enclaves of Single Tax Or Economic Rent: Being a Compendium of the Legal Documents Involved Together with a Historical Description*, Volume 1 (Fiske Warren: Harvard, Mass).

Hyde, Lewis. 1979. *The gift: imagination and the erotic life of property* Random House: New York).

Hyde, Lewis. 2010. *Common as air : revolution, art, and ownership* (Farrar, Straus and Giroux: New York).

Hyndman, Henry. 1911. *The record of an adventurous life* (MacMillan: London).

Inman, Robert P. and Feldstein, Martin S (eds). 1977. *The Economics of Public Services: Proceedings of a Conference held by the International Economic Association - International Economic Association Series.* (Palgrave Macmillan: London).

International Accounting Standards Board. IAS 7 Statement of Cash Flows 2021. https://www.ifrs.org/issued-standards/list-of-standards/ias-7-statement-of-cash-flows/

International Monetary Fund. 2003. World economic outlook: growth and institutions. https://www.imf.org/en/Publications/WEO/Issues/2016/12/31/Growth-and-Institutions

International Monetary Fund. Global Financial Stability Report: Responding to the Financial Crisis and Measuring Systemic Risks. 2009. https://www.imf.org/en/Publications/GFSR/Issues/2016/12/31/Global-Financial-Stability-Report-April-2009-Responding-to-the-Financial-Crisis-and-22583

IPCC AR4 Climate Change 2007: synthesis report https://www.ipcc.ch/report/ar4/syr/

Jackson, Tim. 2009/11. *Prosperity without growth: economics for a finite planet* (Earthscan: London).

Jacobs, Jane. 1961/1992. *The death and life of great American cities* (Random House: New York).

Jacobs, Jane. 1992. *Systems of survival: a dialogue on the moral foundations of commerce and politics* (Random House: New York).

Jansen, M 'A fair share.' *Property week* October 24 2003.

John of Paris 1303. *Tractatus de Potestate Regia et Papali* quoted by Schlatter, Richard. 1951. in *Private property: The history of an idea.* (George Allen & Unwin: London).

Johnson, Robb. *6B go swimming* in Margaret Thatcher: my part in her downfall. 2000. Irregular Records.

Jorgenson, Dale & Yun, Kun-Young. 'The excess burden of taxation in the United States.' *Journal of accounting, auditing and finance.* 6 (1991).

Kaldor, Mary, Martin, Mary, Selchow, Sabine. 2007. *Human security: a new strategic narrative for Europe* (Royal Institute of International Affairs, Chatham House: London).

Kant, Immanuel. 1781. *Metaphysics of morals.*

Kant, Immanuel, and H. Calderwood. 1871. *The metaphysics of ethics* (T. & T. Clark).

Kant, Immanuel. 1930. *Lectures on ethics* (Methuen and Co Ltd: [S.l.]) quoted in Selbourne, David. 2001. *Principle of duty.* (Notre Dame Press: Notre Dame Ind.).

Kaufmann D, Kraay A & Mastruzzi M. 2005. Governance matters IV: Governance indicators for 1994-2004: Policy research working paper 3630. (World Bank: Washington DC).

Kennedy, Paul M. 1987. *The rise and fall of the great powers: economic change and military conflict from 1500 to 2000* (Random House: New York).

Kennickell, A. 2007. 'The Role of Over-sampling of the Wealthy' in the Survey of Consumer Finances, Federal Reserve Board Survey of Consumer Finances Working Papers. https://www.federalreserve.gov/econresdata/scf/files/isi2007.pdf

Kenyatta, Jomo. 1938/1992. *Facing Mount Kenya. The tribal life of the Gikuyu, etc.* (Kenway Publications: Nairobi).

Kerr, Gavin. 2017 *The Property-Owning Democracy: Freedom and Capitalism in the Twenty-First Century* (Routledge: New York and Abingdon, Oxon).

Keynes, John Maynard. 1936. *The general theory of employment, interest*
90

and money (Macmillan: London).

Keynes, John Maynard, and D. E. Moggridge. 1973. *The collected writings of John Maynard Keynes. Vol.14, The General theory and after* (Macmillan for the Royal Economic Society, 1987: London).

Klemperer, Paul. 2004. *Auctions : theory and practice* (Princeton University Press: Princeton, N.J. ; Woodstock).

Kolstad, Charles. 1999. *Environmental economics* (Oxford University Press: New York).

Krutilla, John. Conservation reconsidered, *American Economic Review* 57 (1967) 777-786.

Kurlansky, Mark. 1997. *Cod : a biography of the fish that changed the world* (Alfred A. Knopf Canada: Toronto).

Kuttner, Robert. 1996. *Everything for sale: the virtues and limits of markets* (University of Chicago Press: Chicago).

Kyoto protocol 1997 https://unfccc.int/kyoto_protocol

Lanchester, John. 2010. *Whoops! : why everyone owes everyone and no one can pay* (Penguin: London).

Land Value Tax working party Oxford Oxfordshire County Council. 2005. 'The Oxfordshire Land Value Tax Study' (Oxfordshire County Council: Oxford).

Lange G M & Wright M. 2004. *Sustainable development in mineral economics: the example of Botswana* Environment and Development Economics 9 (4) 485-505 (London: Penguin Press) 67.

Layard, Richard. 2005. *Happiness: lessons from a new science* (Allen Lane: London).

Lefmann, Ole 2017. 'A review of the Danish Henry George Foundation 1902 – 2017.' Lecture to the Henry George Foundation of Great Britain, London 3 November 2017.

LeGrain, Philip. 'Tax land – it can't be hidden from the Revenue.' *Times*. 17 June 2010).

Leopold, Aldo. 1949/1968. *A Sand County Almanac* (Oxford University Press: Oxford).

Locke, John. 1689. *Two treatises on government. By John Locke* (London) https://www.gutenberg.org/files/7370/7370-h/7370-h.htm

Locke, J. 1690/1952) *Concerning civil government: second essay* (a) II,25 and (b) I,42.

Lockwood, Matthew, Bird, Jenny and Alvarez, Raquel. 2007. *2050 vision: How can the UK play its part in avoiding dangerous climate change?* (Institute for Public Policy Research: London).

Lomborg, Bjørn. 2001. *The skeptical environmentalist: measuring the real state of the world* (Cambridge University Press: Cambridge, U.K.).

Lord, Clive, Kennet, Miriam and Felton, Judith. 2011. *Citizens' income and green economics* (Green Economics Institute: Reading).

Lovelock, James. 1979. *Gaia: a new look at life on earth* (Oxford University Press: Oxford).

Lukes, Steven. 1974. *Power: a radical view.* (Macmillan: London).

MacDonald, James, 2000. *Licence to call*   Economist   3/6/2000:6.

Maitland, Frederic William. 1908 /1963. *The Constitutional History of England : A course of lectures* (Cambridge University Press: Cambridge).

Malthus, Thomas. 1798. *An Essay on the Principle of Population*   (J. Johnson: London)   http://www.esp.org/books/malthus/population/malthus.pdf

Mamdani, Mahmood. 'The invention of the indigene.' *London Review of Books,* 20 January 2011, *31*-33.

Marmot, Michael, Theodossiou I & Zangelidis, A. 2006. *The social gradient in health: the effect of absolute and relative income on individual's health*   (Centre for European Labour Market Research: Aberdeen).

Marx, Karl. 1844/2000. 'Economic and philosophical manuscripts' in McLellan, D. 2000. *Karl Marx – selected writings.*   (Oxford University Press: Oxford).

92

Marx, Karl & Engels, Friedrich 1848/1967. *The communist manifesto* (Penguin: Harmondsworth).

Marx, Karl. 1867. *Das Capital Book 1.*

Marx, Karl. 1894. *Das Capital Book 3.*

Marx, Karl, Clemens Palme Dutt, Friedrich Engels, Vladimir Il B. ich Works edited translated or with contributions by this Lenin, and Karl Single Works Marx. *Critique of the Gotha Programme ... With appendices by Marx, Engels and Lenin. (Edited by C. P. Dutt.)* (London, printed in U.S.S.R. : Lawrence & Wishart, (1938)).

Maxwell, Dominic, and Anthony Vigor. 2005. *Time for land value tax?* (IPPR: London).

Mayer, Peter, and Alan Pemberton. 2000. *A short history of land registration in England and Wales* (Land Registry: London).

McAuslan, Patrick, and John F. McEldowney. 1985. *Law, legitimacy, and the constitution : essays marking the centenary of Dicey's Law of the Constitution* (Sweet & Maxwell: London).

McBurney, Stuart. 1990. *Ecology into economics won't go.* (Green Books: Bideford).

McClay, S. and Harrison, R. 2004. 'The impact of school zoning on residential house prices in Christchurch', Department of Economics, University of Canterbury, New Zealand.

McDonnell, John 2007. Bring in Land Value Tax to replace Council Tax
http://www.johnmcdonnell.org.uk/2007/03/bring-in-land-value-tax-to-replace.html

McLeay, M, Radia, A., Thomas, R. ' Money creation in the modern economy.' *Bank of England Quarterly Bulletin.* Q1 2014.

McLellan, D. 2000. Karl Marx – selected writings.   Oxford: Oxford University Press.

Meadows, Donella H. 1972. *The limits to growth : a report for the Club of Rome's project on the predicament of mankind* (Potomac Associates: London).

Melchett, Peter. Letter. *Economist,* 13 January 2007, 15.

Metzner, Ralph 1995. *The psychopathology of the human-nature relationship* in Roszak, T., Gomes, M. E., & Kanner, A. D. (Eds.).1995. *Ecopsychology: Restoring the earth, healing the mind.* (Sierra Club Books: San Francisco).

Mill, John Stuart. 1849. *Principles of Political Economy, with some of their applications to Social Philosophy.* (John Parker: London).

Millennium Ecosystem Assessment Conceptual Framework Working Group. 2003. *Ecosystems and human well-being: a framework for assessment.* (Island Press: Washington DC).

Millennium Ecosystem Assessment Board. 2005. *Ecosystems and human well-being: synthesis.* (Island Press: Washington DC).

Mirrlees, James A., and Stuart Adam. 2011. *Tax by design : the Mirrlees review* (Oxford University Press: Oxford).

Monbiot, George, 'Communism, welfare state – what's the next big idea?' *Guardian*, 2 April 2013.

Monbiot, George. 2006. *Heat : how to stop the planet burning* (Allen Lane: London).

Muellbaur, John & Murphy, Anthony. 'Booms and busts in the UK housing market.' *The Economic Journal* 107 (Nov 1997) 1701-1727.

Muellbaur, John 2005. *Property taxation and the economy* in Maxwell, Dominic, and Anthony Vigor. 2005. *Time for land value tax?* (IPPR: London).

Muellbaur, John 2003. 'Housing, credit and the euro: the policy response.' *Economic Outlook* 27:4 July 2003. 5-13.

Murphy, Richard. 2008. *The missing billions : the UK tax gap* (TUC: London).

National Audit Office 2018. *PFI and PF2.* (National Audit Office: London).

National Bureau of Economic Research., and Brookings Institution. 1964. *The Role of direct and indirect taxes in the Federal revenue system; a conference report of the National Bureau of Economic Research and the Brookings Institution* (Princeton University Press: Princeton N.J.).

National Land and Property Gazetteer. 2014. https://data.gov.uk/dataset/9231ef97-a965-4d91-97c4-482d33de459a/national-land-and-property-gazetteer

National Research University Higher School of Economics. 2018. *Why economic growth does not necessarily contribute to human happiness* https://phys.org/news/2018-03-economic-growth-necessarily-contribute-human.html

Nelissen, Dagmar asper & Faber, Jasper. 2012. *Costs and Benefits of Stopping the Clock: How Airlines Profit from Changes in the EU ETS.* (Delft CE: Delft).

New Economics Foundation. 2003. *Limits to property: the failure of restrictive property regimes in the modern world.* (New Economics Foundation: London).

New Zealand Treasury, 2005. Cost Benefit Analysis Primer, Version 1.12.

Nigel, Richard Fitz (b 1176) *Dialoguo de Saccario* (Dialogue concerning the exchequer) Galbraith, John Kenneth, Frank Moraes, and Edward Horne. 1974. *John Kenneth Galbraith introduces India* (Deutsch: London).

Norregaard, John. 2013. Taxing immovable property: revenue potential and implementation challenges: IMF Working Paper.

Nozick, Robert. 1974. *Anarchy, State and Utopia.* (Basic Books: New York).

Nuti, Domenico Mario and Nove, Alex (eds.). 1972. *Socialist economics: selected readings.* (Penguin: Harmondsworth).

OECD. 2010. Tax policy reform and economic growth: Paris OECD tax policy studies No 20.

Office for National Statistics. 1998. National accounts: concepts, sources and methods. (Office for National Statistics: London).

Office for National Statistics. 2009. United Kingdom national accounts: the blue book (Palgrave MacMillan: Basingstoke).

Office for National Statistics 2017 UK House Price Index 2017 https://www.ons.gov.uk/economy/inflationandpriceindices/bulletins/housepriceindex/jan2017

Office for National Statistics 2017a. Unpaid carers provide social care worth £57 billion. https://www.ons.gov.uk/peoplepopulationandcommunity/healthandsocialcare/healthandlifeexpectancies/articles/unpaidcarersprovidesocialcareworth57billion/2017-07-10

Ogilvie, William 1782/1920. The right of property in land in Beer, Max. 1920. *History of British Socialism. (*G.Bell & Sons: London).

Olmer, Naya et al. 2017. Greenhouse gas emissions from global shipping, 2013 – 2015. International Council on Clean Transportation.

Oreskes, Naomi. 2004. The scientific consensus on climate change. *Science* 306, 3 December 2004. 1686.

Ormerod, Paul. 1994. *The death of economics.*(Faber & Faber: London).

Ostrom, Elinor. 1990. Governing the commons: the evolution of institutions for collective action (Cambridge University Press: Cambridge).

Oswald, Andrew. A conjecture on the explanation of high unemployment in the industrialised nations: Warwick Economic Research Paper 1996 475.

Oxfordshire Land Value Tax Working Party. 2005. The Oxfordshire Land Value Tax Study. www.labourland.org/downloads/papers/oxfordshire_land_value_tax_study.pdf

PAC (House of Commons Committee of Public Accounts). H M Revenue & Customs: PAYE, Tax Credit debt and cost reductions. 20 December 2011. (The Stationery Office: London).

Paine, Thomas. 1797 a. *Agrarian Justice.* (T G Ballard: London).

Paine, Thomas 2017 *Agrarian Justice* (Lulu).

Paine, Thomas (Thomas Payne). 1797b. *A la législature et au directoire exécutif de la republique Francaise* (Ragouleau: Paris).

Paine, Thomas 1802 / 2017. *Proposal that Louisiana be purchased.* (Lulu).

Paine, Thomas, and Moncure Daniel Conway. 1894. *The Writings of Thomas Paine. Collected and edited by M. D. Conway* (G. P. Putnam's Sons: New York).

96

Parker, Hermione. 1989. *Instead of the dole: an enquiry into the integration of the tax and benefit systems.* (Routledge: London).

Patten, Alan. 'Hegel's Justification Of Private Property.' *History of Political Thought*, 16 4, 1995, 576–600.

Payne, Raymond. 24 February 2012. Talk to Henry George Foundation, London.

Pearce, David W. 1993. *Blueprint 3 : measuring sustainable development* (Earthscan: London).

Pearce, Fred. 2006. When the rivers run dry: What happens when our water runs out? (Eden Project Books: London).

Penguin Books. 1972. *Socialist Economics.* (Penguin: Harmondsworth).

Pensions Commission. 2006. A New Pension Settlement for the Twenty-First Century: The Second Report of the Pensions Commission. https://webarchive.nationalarchives.gov.uk/+/http:/www.dwp.gov.uk/publications/dwp/2005/pensionscommreport/main-report.pdf

Phang, Sock-Yong. 2000. 'Hong Kong and Singapore' in Andelson, Robert (ed). 2000. Land value taxation around the world (Blackwells: Oxford).

Pickard, Duncan. 2004. Lie of the land: a study in the culture of deception. (Shepheard-Walwyn: London).

Plato and Jowett. 360BC/2016. *The Laws of Plato.* (CreateSpace Independent Publishing Platform).

Plato and Lee, H., 375BC/1974. *The Republic.* (Penguin: Harmondsworth).

Plimmer, Frances & Sayce, Sarah. 2006. Depreciated Replacement Cost – Consistent Methodology? Munich, XXIII FIC Congress https://www.fig.net/resources/proceedings/fig_proceedings/fig2006/papers/ts86/ts86_01_plimmer_sayce_0268.pdf

Plimmer, Frances. 1998. Rating law and valuation: a practical guide (Addison Wesley Longman: London).

Pope Leo XIII 1891. *Rerum Novarum*. Encyclical On Capital And Labour
https://www.vatican.va/content/leo-xiii/en/encyclicals/documents/hf_l-xiii_enc_15051891_rerum-novarum.html

Potter J, Moore B. 'UK Enterprise Zones and the Attraction of Inward Investment'. *Urban Studies*.37(8. 2000:1279-1311.

Pratt, Julian. 201, 2022. *Stewardship economy: private property without private ownership*. First edition, second edition (Lulu).

Pratt, Julian. 2014. *Supporting local economies: from Business Rates to Land Value Taxation* (Lulu).

Pratt, Julian. 2017. *An approach to resolving territorial conflict* in *Paine, Thomas* 1802 / 2017. *Proposal that Louisiana be purchased* (Lulu).

Pratt, Julian. 2022. *Stewardship Economy 2: Valuing land and managing transition* (Lulu).

Pratt, Julian. 2022. *Stewardship Economy 3: Land, environment and climate* (Lulu).

Pratt, Julian. 2022. *Stewardship Economy 4: The economy, wealth and universal income* (Lulu).

Pratt, Julian. 2022. *Stewardship Economy 5: Efficient, fair taxes and the role of the state* (Lulu).

Pratt, Julian. 2022. *Stewardship Economy 6: Property rights* (Lulu).

Pratt, Julian. 2022. *Stewardship Economy 7: Economic terms explained and bibliography* (Lulu).

Pritchett, Lant. 'Divergence, Big Time.' *Journal of Economic Perspectives* 11:3 (summer 1997) 3-17.

Proudhon, P. J., Bonnie G. Smith, and Donald R. Kelley. 1994. *What is property?* (Cambridge University Press: Cambridge).

Proudhon, Pierre-Joseph. 1840/1994. *What is property?* (Cambridge University Press: Cambridge).

Pufendorf, Samuel. 1672. *The law of nature and nations* translated Kennett 1729, (Basil & Carew).

Purves, Andrew 2015. *No debt, high growth, low tax: Hong Kong's economic miracle explained* Shepheard Walwyn: London).

Putnam, Robert G., Frank J. Taylor, and Phillip G. Kettle. 1970. *A geography of urban places* (Routledge, 2007: London).

Quesnay, François. 1758/1894. *Tableau œconomique* (British Economic Association: London) Facsimile, in French.

Quesnay, François 1760 / 1846. 'Maximes générales de gouvernement economique d'un royaume agricole, et notes sure ces maxims' in M Eugène Daire, *Physiocrates*. Réimpression de l'éd. 1846.

Qulligan, James. 'People Sharing Resources | Toward a New Multilateralism of the Global Commons' *Kosmos* (2009) https://www.kosmosjournal.org/article/people-sharing-resources-toward-a-new-multilateralism-of-the-global-commons

Ramsey, Frank 'A contribution to the theory of taxation.' *Economic Journal* (1927) 47-61.

Ratha, Dilip. Workers' Remittances: An Important and Stable Source of External Development Finance *Global Development Finance*, April 2003, https://papers.ssrn.com/sol3/papers.cfm?abstract_id=3201568

Rawls, John. 1972. *A theory of justice* (Clarendon Press: Oxford).

Ricardo, David. 1817. *On the principles of political economy, and taxation:1* (John Murray: London).

Richards, David. 1989. *Land Value of Britain, 1985-90* (Economic & Social Science Research Association).

Royal Institute of Chartered Surveyors (RICS). 2006. *Valuation Information Paper 9: land and building apportionments for lease classification under international financial reporting standards* (Royal Institute of Chartered Surveyors: London).

Royal Institute of Chartered Surveyors (RICS). 2009. *RICS Valuation standards (Red book)* (Royal Institute of Chartered Surveyors: London).

Ridley, Matt. 1996/1997. *The origins of virtue.* (Penguin: Harmondsworth).

Riley, Don. 2001. *Taken for a Ride: Taxpayers, Trains and HM Treasury.* Centre for Land Policy Studies.

Ringen, Stein. 2007. *What democracy is for: on freedom and moral government* (Princeton University Press: Princeton).

Robertson, James. 1994. *Benefits and taxes: a radical strategy.* (New Economics Foundation: London).

Robertson, James. 2009. *G20 monetary campaign: crash campaign* www.jamesrobertson.com/g20monetaryreform.pdf

Robertson, James. 2012. *Future Money Breakdown or breakthrough?* (Green Books: Totnes, Devon).

Roche, Barbara 1998. *Written answer to parliamentary question 18th May.* (Hansard: London).

Romer, Paul M. 'Increasing Returns and Long-Run Growth' *Journal of Political Economy.* 94:5 (Oct. 1986), 1002-1037.

Ronald Banks. 1998. 'The people's stake: resource rents and the UK budget', in Fred Harrison *The losses of nations : deadweight politics versus public rent dividends,* (Othila: London).

Rosselson, Leon. 1975. The world turned upside down on *That's not the way it's got to be.* Acorn Records.

Roszak, Theodore, Gomes, Mary & Kanner, Allen (eds) 1995. *Ecopsychology: Restoring the earth, healing the mind,* San Francisco, Sierra Club Books.

Rothbard, Murray. 1957. *The single tax: economic and moral implications.* New York Foundation for Economic Education.

Rothbard, Murray. 1974. 'Justice & property rights' in Blumenfeld, Samuel.

Rousseau, Jean-Jacques. 1755. 'Discourse on the origins of inequality' in Cole 1973.

Roy, Rana. 2004. Not By Spending Alone: The Case For A Comprehensive Tax Review, Report for the Railway Forum, London, co-sponsored by the Robert Schalkenbach Foundation, New York, NY.

Royal Institute of Chartered Surveyors 1994. Understanding the property cycle (Royal Institute of Chartered Surveyors: London).

Ryan, Alan. 1984. *Property and political theory* (Blackwell: Oxford).

Ryan-Collins, Josh, Greenham, Tony, Werner, Richard, Jackson, Andrew. 2011. *Where Does Money Come From? A guide to the UK monetary and banking system.* (New Economics Foundation: London).

Saunders Peter. 2010. *Beware False Prophets: Equality, the Good Society and the Spirit Level* (London: Policy Exchange).

Sachs, Jeffrey. Nature, nurture and growth *Economist.* June 14, 1997, 21-23.

Samuelson, P. 'The gains from international trade once again.' *Economic Journal* 72 (1962) 820-829.

Samuelson, Paul & Nordhaus, William 1992 (14th edition)) *Economics* New York McGraw-Hill.

Schlatter, Richard. 1951. *Private property: The history of an idea.* (George Allen & Unwin: London).

Schumacher, E. F. 1973/1974. *Small is beautiful: a study of economics as if people mattered.* (Abacus: London).

Schumpeter, Joseph A. 1939. *Business cycles; a theoretical, historical, and statistical analysis of the capitalist process* (McGraw-Hill Book Company, inc.: New York, London).

Schumpeter, Joseph. 1942. *Capitalism, Socialism and Democracy* (Harper and Bros: New York).

Scottish Government. 2008. Scottish vacant and derelict land survey 2007. https://www.webarchive.org.uk/wayback/archive/20150219015227/http://www.gov.scot/Publications/2008/01/241 50145/0

Selbourne, David. 2001. *Principle of duty.* (Notre Dame Press: Notre Dame Ind.).

Select Committee on Environmental Audit. 2008 Environmental audit: third report. https://publications.parliament.uk/pa/cm200708/cmselect/cmenvaud/149/14912.htm

Shaxson, Nicholas. 2007. *Poisoned wells: the dirty politics of African oil* (Palgrave Macmillan: London).

Shoard, M. 1987. *This Land is Our Land* (Grafton Books, Paladin Imprint: London).

Shoard, Marion. 1997. *This land is our land : the struggle for Britain's countryside* (Gaia: London).

Sijm, Joset al 2005. CO_2 price dynamics: the implications of EU emissions trading for the price of electricity. (Energy research centre of the Netherlands) https://inis.iaea.org/search/search.aspx?orig_q=RN:36113036

Skouras, Athanassios. Land and its taxation as issues in economic theory: what is the reason for their eclipse? *The American Journal of Economics and Sociology* 39:4 (October 1980) 373-382 https://www.jstor.org/stable/3486272

Smith, Adam. 1776. *An inquiry into the nature and causes of the wealth of nations.* (Whitestone et al.: Dublin).

Smolka, M.O. 2013. *Implementing Value Capture in Latin America: Policies and Tools for Urban Development* (Lincoln Institute of Land Policy: Cambridge, MA).

Solnicka, Sara J. and Hemenway, David. 'Is more always better?: A survey on positional concerns' *Journal of Economic Behavior & Organization* 37 (1998) 373 -383.

Soto, Hernando de. 2001. *The mystery of capital : why capitalism triumphs in the West and fails everywhere else* (Black Swan: London).

Spence, Thomas 1776. *Property in Land Every One's Right,* proved in a lecture read to the Philosophical Society in Newcastle on 8th Nov 1775 www.thomas-spence-society.co.uk/debates-the-northumbrian-enlightenment/

Spence, Thomas. 1796. *The meridian sun of liberty; or, the whole rights of man displayed, and most accurately defined.*

Spence, Thomas. (unknown) Essay on printing.

Spencer, Herbert. 1851. *Social Statics: or the Conditions essential to Human Happiness specified, and the first of them developed* (John Chapman: London).

Starhawk. 1982. *Dreaming the dark : magic, sex & politics* (Unwin Hyman: London).

Steiner, Hillel. 1994. *An essay on rights.* (Blackwell: Oxford).

Stern, Nicholas 2007. The economics of climate change: The Stern review (Cambridge University Press: Cambridge).

Sternam, John, D. Teaching Takes Off: Flight Simulators for Management Education. "The Beer Game." *OR/MS Today*, October 1992, 40-44.

Stewart, John. 2010. *Prime minister* (Shepheard-Walwyn: London).

Sully, Rob 'Schools business rates policy is labelled perverse' *Carmarthern Journal,* 3 August 2011.

Taleb, Nassim Nicholas. 2007. *Fooled by randomness : the hidden role of chance in life and in the markets* (Penguin: London).

Thane, P. 2005. 'The 'scandal' of women's pensions in Britain: how did it come about?' http://www.historyandpolicy.org/policy-papers/papers/the-scandal-of-womens-pensions-in-britain-how-did-it-come-about

Tideman, Nicolaus. 1994. *Land and taxation* (Shepheard-Walwyn in association with Centre for Incentive Taxation: London).

Tideman, N. & Plassman, F. 1998. Taxed out of work and wealth: the costs of taking labour and capital. in Harrison, F. (2006) *Wheels of fortune* (Institute of Economic Affairs: London).

Tideman, Nicolaus 2004. The Case for Taxing Land. Virginia Polytechnic Institute & State University Working Paper http://www.wealthandwant.com/docs/Tideman_CTL.html

TimeBank https://timebank.org.uk/

Tobin, James, and P. M. Jackson. 1987. *Policies for prosperity: essays in a Keynesian mode* (Wheatsheaf: Brighton).

Toíbín, Colm London Review of Books 1998 https://www.lrb.co.uk/the-paper/v20/n15/colm-toibin/erasures

Tomson, Aivar 2001. 'Estonia' in Andelson, Robert (ed). 2000. *Land value taxation around the world* (Oxford:Blackwells).

Torry, Malcolm. 2009. Can unconditional cash transfers work? They can. Citizen's Income Trust Newsletter 2 https://citizensincome.org/news/citizens-income-newsletter-2009-issue-2/

Townsend, Peter & Davidson, Nick (eds). 1982. *Inequalities in health: the Black report.* (Pelican: London).

Toynbee, P. & Walker, D. 2008. *Unjust rewards: exposing greed and inequality in Britain today* (Granta: London) 77.

Toynbee, Polly. All Labour needs to summon is nerve, daring and ambition *Guardian* 7 September 2009 www.theguardian.com/commentisfree/2009/sep/07/labour-radical-ideas-electoral-reform

Trades Union Congress (TUC) 2011. Conference Decisions 2011, Alternative Economic Strategy.

Tudge, Colin. 2004. *So shall we reap : what's gone wrong with the world's food - and how to fix it* (Penguin: London).

Tully, James. 1980. *A discourse on property: John Locke and his adversaries.* (Cambridge University Press: Cambridge, U.K.).

Turgot, Anne-Robert-Jacques. 1788. *Reflexions sur la Formation et la Distribution des Richesses.*

Turner, Graham. 2008. A comparison of The Limits to Growth with 30 years of reality. *Global Environmental Change* 18 412-414.

UK National Accounts, The Blue Book time series 2016-20.

Union of the Physically Impaired against Segregation and the Disability Alliance (1976) Fundamental Principles of Disability. https://disability-studies.leeds.ac.uk/wp-content/uploads/sites/40/library/UPIAS-fundamental-principles.pdf

United Nations 1948. Universal declaration of human rights. https://www.un.org/en/universal-declaration-human-rights/

United Nations Framework Convention on Climate Change https://unfccc.int/process-and-meetings/the-convention/what-is-the-united-nations-framework-convention-on-climate-change

Valuation Office Agency. 2010. 2013a. 2013b. https://www.gov.uk/government/organisations/valuation-office-agency

Van Parijs, P. 1995/1997. *Real freedom for all: what (if anything) can justify capitalism.* (Clarendon Press: Oxford) (a) 25 (b) 33 (c) 92-99 and note 16, (d) 105.

Vickers, Tony. 2007. *Location matters : recycling Britain's wealth* (Shepheard-Walwyn: London).

Vickers, Tony. 2009. Visualising the landvaluescape: developing the case for Britain https://eprints.kingston.ac.uk/id/eprint/20232/

Vickrey, William. 1977. 'The city as a firm' in Inman, Robert P. and Feldstein, Martin S (eds). *The Economics of Public Services: Proceedings of a Conference held by the International Economic Association - International Economic Association Series.* (Palgrave Macmillan: London).

Vickrey, William. 1995. 'Simplification, progression and a level playing field.' reprinted in Wenzer, Kenneth C. 1999. *Land-value taxation : the equitable and efficient source of public finance* (Shepheard-Walwyn: London).

Vidal, John & Carroll, Rory, 'Ecuador signs $3.6bn deal not to exploit oil-rich Amazon reserve', *Guardian,* 5 August 2011.

Victor, Peter. 2008. *Managing Without Growth: Slower by Design, Not Disaster* (Advances in Ecological Economics series). (Edward Elgar Publishing Ltd: Cheltenham).

von Mises. 1972. 'Economic calculation' in Nuti, Domenico Mario and Nove, Alex (eds.). 1972. *Socialist economics: selected readings.* (Penguin: Harmondsworth).

Wadsworth, Mark. 2006. *Tax, benefits, pensions: keep it simple Part 2: ten steps to simplicity* Bow Group.

Wadsworth, Mark. 2013. https://markwadsworth.blogspot.com/search?q=2013

Waldron, Jeremy. 1987. *'Nonsense upon stilts': Bentham, Burke and Marx on the rights of man* (Methuen: London).

Waldron, Jeremy. 1988. *The right to private property* (Clarendon: Oxford).

Weitzman ML, Spence AM. 'Regulatory Strategies for Pollution Control.' in: Friedlaender, A.F. *Approaches to Controlling Air Pollution*. Vol. April 1978. (M.I.T. Press: Cambridge, MA).

Weitzman, Martin. 1974. Prices versus quantities.   *Rev Econ Studies,* quoted in Kolstad, 186.

Wenzer, Kenneth C. 1999. *Land-value taxation : the equitable and efficient source of public finance* (Shepheard-Walwyn: London).

Wetzel, Dave. 2013. *Land Value Tax with residential exemptions* (personal communication).

White, Huntingdon Charles. 1922. *Enclaves of Single Tax (or Economic Rent): being a compendium of the legal documents involved, together with a historical description [for the year 1920, etc.]* (Fiske Warren, 1921: Harvard).

White, Stuart. 1997. Liberal Equality, Exploitation, and the Case for an Unconditional Basic Income. *Political Studies* 45: 2, June 1, 1997, 312-326.

Whittemore, Claire C. *Land for People :Land Tenure and the very Poor.* Oxfam Public Affairs Unit, 1981 - Developing countries.

Widerquist, K. & Arndt, G. 2020. The Cost of Basic Income in the United Kingdom: A Microsimulation Analysis. https://www.semanticscholar.org/paper/The-Cost-of-Basic-Income-in-the-United-Kingdom%3A-A-Widerquist-Arndt/af51e4180f6c0a5baf1fd2ff22c6a8849b9b77b0

Wightman, Andy. 2011. *The poor had no lawyers : who owns Scotland (and how they got it)* (Birlinn: Edinburgh).

Wilkinson, Richard. 2005. *The Impact of Inequality: How to Make Sick Societies Healthier.* (Routledge: Abingdon).

Wilks, Hector. 1964. Rating of site values: report of a pilot survey at Whitstable. (Rating and Valuing Association: London).

Wilks, Hector 1974. Site Value Rating: report on a research carried out in the town of Whitstable. (The Land Institute: London).

Wilks, Hector M. 1984. *Principles and practice of rating valuation* (Estate Gazette: London).

Williams, Jonty 2014. Husbandry: an ancient art for the modern world. (Lulu).

Williams, R Gwyn 2008 (4th edn)) Agricultural valuations: a practical guide. London Estates Gazette.

Winstanley, Gerrard. 1649. *A Declaration from the poor oppressed people of England, directed to all that call themselves Lords of Manors, ... that have begun to ... cut, or ... do intend to cut down the woods and trees that grow upon the Commons and waste land.* (London).

Winstanley, Gerrard. 1649. *A watchword to the City of London and the Armie: wherein you may see that England's freedome which should be the result of all our victories is sinking deeper under the Norman power, as appears by this relation of the proceedings of Kingstone-Court against some of the Diggers at George-Hill, under colour of law, etc* (Calvert: London).

Winstanley,   Gerrard.   1649.   *New   law   of   righteousness.* https://www.diggers.org/diggers-ENGLISH-1649/NEW-LAW-OF-RIGHTEOUSNESS-1648-Winstanley.pdf

Wolf, Martin. Why we must halt the land cycle. *Financial Times* July 8th, 2010.

World Bank. 1978. Urban land policy: issues and opportunities   World Bank Staff Working Paper No. 283   quoted in McAuslan, Patrick, and John F. McEldowney. 1985. *Law, legitimacy, and the constitution : essays marking the centenary of Dicey's Law of the Constitution* (Sweet & Maxwell: London).

World Commission for Development and Environment of the United Nations. 1987. *Our common future (the Brundland report).* (Oxford paperbacks: Oxford).